Praise for

Bylines and Blessings

"The best successful journalism is, by definition, timely. Religious values, in their very essence, are timeless. Judy Gruen explores the contradictory and occasionally complementary passions that have driven her eventful life with insight and humor. For the reader, her perspective can deepen faith at the same time that it enhances appreciation for the writer's craft."

—Michael Medved, Syndicated Talk Show Host, Author of *The American Miracle*

"Gruen is an effortlessly good writer, an effortlessly funny writer, and an effortlessly deep writer, though there is nothing effortless about writing. Though I'm a soldier of the nefarious left, and as secular as a Jew can be while still retaining membership, I respect her points of view and her passion. My endorsement of *Bylines and Blessings* is from the heart."

—Howard Rosenberg, Author, *Blizzard of Lies*, Pulitzer Prize–Winning Author and Journalist

"Gruen tackles issues I've thought about but never dared to make public, and I'm grateful for her relatable voice and courage. *Bylines and Blessings* is for writers of books, letters, social media posts, and anyone seeking to understand how to live life with gentle balance."

—Laya Saul, Author of *Sisterhood of the Copper Mirrors: The Legacy of the Jewish Woman*

"*Bylines and Blessings* is that rare book that I can't wait to get back to. It's smart, funny, interesting, deep, charming, honest, brave, and real. It's the journey of a person fighting to grow, change, shed old skin, and constantly become new. It's the story of an artist struggling for her art, humanity, spiritual life, and doing what's right for her family. You'll laugh, cry, and learn the many blessings you may not have known you already possess. I loved it."

—Mark Schiff, Author of *Why Not? Lessons in Courage, Comedy and Chutzpah*

"A Jewish journalist is not so different from a Christian journalist where faith and ambition bump up against each other. Gruen tells the stories of hard life lessons with engaging humor and reveals that with faith, grit, and love of God and family, life does indeed offer resounding success."

—Patti Maguire Armstrong, Best-Selling Author of the Children's "Dear God" Series, Journalist at *National Catholic Register*

"Judy Gruen has a wonderful writing style—evocative and humorous. She shows her path to a life that I think all spiritual seekers are after but which can get lost when we make the search all about *me* when it's really all about *us*."

—Jennifer Lawler, Author of *Dojo Wisdom*

"As someone who spent forty years as a journalist, I understand the daily battles to not only get the story but to get it right. Judy Gruen also understands this and writes about her fascinating career with humor, depth, and poignancy."

—Matthew Schwartz, Eight-Time Emmy and Murrow Award–Winning Reporter, Author of *Confessions of an Investigative Reporter*

"*Bylines and Blessings* made me think about my own life, and I cheered as Gruen relied on her humor, heart, and strong belief in the Jewish faith to bring her through personal and professional struggles. Five stars!"

> —Carrie Scarborough Kinnard, Author of *From the Grit Comes a Pearl: A Southern Woman's Imperfect Faith in Her God, in Herself, and in Her Humorous, Unique Outlook on Life's Stumbling Blocks*

"Judy Gruen's memoir will inspire anyone struggling to build a career . . . and a life. I would've enjoyed it immensely no matter what work she chose to pursue, but it's especially fun to learn how this talented writer evolved her craft and turned her passion into her profession while always remaining true to her faith and values. Highly recommended!"

> —Salvador Litvak, Director of *Man in the Long Black Coat*, Influencer at *Accidental Talmudist*

"Judy Gruen has long explored her faith through her writing, and she ties the two together seamlessly in *Bylines and Blessings*. It's a wholly satisfying read that breaks down stereotypes about Orthodox women (and men) interwoven with timeless Jewish teachings."

> —Chaplain Rachel C. Weingarten, Author of *Ancient Prayer: Channeling Your Faith 365 Days of the Year*

"Judy Gruen invites readers on an unfiltered journey through the peaks and valleys of her career and spiritual exploration, blending humor and inspiration for a memoir that's as entertaining as it is enlightening."

> —Arty Cweiber, Editor of *Shabbos Reads*, *18Forty*

Also by Judy Gruen

The Skeptic and the Rabbi: Falling in Love with Faith

Till We Eat Again: A Second Helping

MBA Admissions for Smarties: The No-Nonsense Guide to Acceptance at Top Business Schools (with Linda Abraham)

The Women's Daily Irony Supplement

Carpool Tunnel Syndrome: Motherhood as Shuttle Diplomacy

Bylines and Blessings:
Overcoming Obstacles, Striving for Excellence,
and Redefining Success

by Judy Gruen

© Copyright 2024 Judy Gruen

ISBN 979-8-88824-240-7

All rights reserved. No part of this publication may be reproduced, stored in a retrieval system, or transmitted in any form or by any means—electronic, mechanical, photocopy, recording, or any other—except for brief quotations in printed reviews, without the prior written permission of the author.

Excerpt from Elizabeth Berg's *The Year of Pleasures: A Novel,* granted by Penguin Random House

Published by

3705 Shore Drive
Virginia Beach, VA 23455
800-435-4811
www.koehlerbooks.com

Bylines and Blessings

OVERCOMING OBSTACLES, STRIVING FOR EXCELLENCE, AND REDEFINING SUCCESS

JUDY GRUEN

VIRGINIA BEACH
CAPE CHARLES

For Ahuva, Leeba Leah, Herschel, Reuven, Dovi, Yaakov Moshe, Miriam, Aron, Ezra, Libby, and Chana Etty. Boundless love.

Table of Contents

Author's Note 5

Young, Fearless, and Foolish 10

With Ink-Stained Hands 17

Learning the "Trades" 28

Hard-Won Lessons in Humor Writing 41

Interviewing "The Big Man" 47

Chasing Bylines from Westwood to Washington, DC 54

Planning a Career, Planning a Life 66

The Community and the Corporation 76

Writing Against the Societal Tides 86

My Fifteen Minutes of Writing About Fame 93

Author! Author! 99

Crises 107

Kosher Dilemmas 114

Ruff Love with My Third Book 119

Responsibilities 128

Standing Room Only 134

Boundaries 140

Follow the Blessing 145

Responding to the Jewish Misery Memoir Market 154

Politics and the Writing World 163

More Blessings 178

Column Fodder on Aisle 9! 183

Still Navigating the Joyful Chaos of Working from Home 188

From Generation to Generation 193

Acknowledgments 197

Author's Note

Truth takes time...
—Robert Caro, *Working*

One Saturday morning when I was eight years old, my grandmother and I sat down to breakfast at her kitchen table. Cece and I weren't blood relatives—she was my paternal grandfather's second wife, but I considered her my grandmother in every way. With no natural children of her own, she considered me her granddaughter as well. A health-conscious vegetarian, Cece took dainty bites from her standard morning fare: two thick slices of dark, whole-grain bread studded with pumpkin and other healthy seeds, and strong black coffee. I had a kid-friendly bowl of some kid-friendly, sugar-laden cereal.

On weekends, I often slept over at my grandparents' modest but lovely home in Pacific Palisades. On Saturday mornings after breakfast, Cece would drive my grandfather Papa Rosenfeld and me to her office in a two-story office building on Sunset Boulevard. Cece had built a thriving practice as a homeopathic physician and acupuncturist, and as she treated patients, I sat happily in the waiting room, chatting with those still waiting for the nurse to call them in. Born of either a reporter's instinct—or simple nosiness—I loved asking these strangers about themselves. Given that it was only 1968, most of Cece's patients were avant-garde or medically progressive thinkers, including a sprinkling of Hollywood celebrities. I remember everyone being very friendly to me. Of course, they probably didn't want any bad reports floating back to their doctor, either—she decided where to stick those acupuncture needles.

That morning as we were finishing our breakfast, Cece said, "Judy, when you grow up I know you're going to be a writer." A thrill pulsed through me. No one else—not anyone in my family nor any teacher—had made that prediction. Cece validated what I already felt in the deepest part of myself.

My grandmother's daring professional choices as a woman from her generation, coupled with her belief in me, buoyed my confidence. During college, I saw my chance to begin writing for publication through Jewish campus journalism. That influence came from my maternal grandparents, Rabbi Bernard and Ethel Cohen, as well as a wealth of positive experiences in Jewish youth groups, camps, and synagogue. I wrote extensively about my pair of wildly opposite grandparents in my first memoir, *The Skeptic and the Rabbi: Falling in Love With Faith*. Despite their polar opposite personalities, lifestyles, and value systems, their influence on me was profound—Jewishly and professionally. I found them endlessly fascinating, and I loved them all very much.

The Skeptic and the Rabbi was my heartfelt response to the numerous memoirs written by formerly Orthodox writers who had left that life. Several were published in a span of a few years, most to great acclaim. The establishment literary culture was and remains heavily biased against traditional faith, and I wrote my memoir out of my own pain in seeing the consistently lopsided and unfair views of Orthodoxy in the media at large, which hungrily sought out any story that could be exploited to show our lifestyle as something dark, oppressive, and forbidding.

I knew there was a far healthier, happier side to living an Orthodox life because I was living it, and so were tens of thousands of others. I felt protective and proud of Torah Judaism and was sick of people bashing it. And so I wrote my memoir, and thought I was done with the writing of memoirs.

But years later, another memoirish story began to bubble up inside me. It was the story about the hard-won lessons throughout my writing life—about persistence and dedication to craft, taking my lumps and trying to learn from them, finding my voice, turning life's absurdities and frustrations into humor columns, and defining and then redefining success.

My Jewish values forged this career development. These values helped me plan not just a career but a life. They kept my priorities straight when my ego and ambition threatened to get the better of me. They helped me keep perspective and from becoming embittered as I felt my voice less and less welcome in the publishing world, where leftist views were increasingly imposed as the only way to think. I felt increasingly like a lone voice in their midst. (But I wasn't alone; several who agreed with me would email privately, saying they were glad *I* spoke up in the discussion boards even if they couldn't.) Humor has always played a huge role in my writing, and I wanted my stories to demonstrate that even after devastating losses, we need to keep writing and reading the funny stuff because humor is not a luxury; it's a life tool.

I began my writing career in the healthcare field, while dabbling in feature and essay work for Jewish media. Over the decades I've written about a wealth of topics from education, psychology, relationships, parenthood, politics, books, movies, and other cultural issues from a Jewish point of view. I've written about personalities as diverse as Rabbi Jonathan Sacks and Bruce Springsteen, a seventeenth-century Jewish memoirist named Glikl of Hamelin, actor Michael Douglas, and Holocaust survivor Dr. Edith Eger. My commentary pieces have appeared in the *Wall Street Journal, Chicago Tribune, Boston Globe,* and the *New York Daily News,* among other outlets. I've ghostwritten and edited memoirs as well as books on Jewish philosophy, alternative health, and business communication. I became a regularly featured writer on *Aish.com* and the *Jewish Journal,* opportunities for which I remain grateful.

Passion is an overused word, but it's an appropriate one to describe my lifelong drive to make my stories come alive through clear, evocative, and vibrant language. I never tire of trying to improve on what I have done before. My drive for excellence always made me careful with the words I chose, but my deepening knowledge of Jewish teachings took it to another level. We create worlds with words, as Rabbi Jonathan Sacks wrote. And we can tear them down with words as well. In our society, so much hurt and pain are caused by reckless use of language—both in speech and in writing. I wanted my work to be part of the solution and not the problem.

As this book went into production, the Jewish world was turned upside down and deeply traumatized by the October 7, 2023 massacres by Hamas terrorists of 1,200 innocent men, women, and children living in Israel (dozens of whom were not Israeli, and some not even Jewish) and the abduction of 240 others, from infants to Holocaust survivors. As Israel fought to destroy this terror organization that also brutalizes its own people, millions around the world rose up to cheer their savagery.

Anti-Semitic incidents had already been skyrocketing throughout the United States and in Europe, including physical assaults on Jews individually. But after October 7, hundreds of thousands gathered in the streets, screaming words of praise for terrorists and words carrying ugly threats against all Jews. We create worlds with words. And we can tear them down with words as well.

Grappling with the shock of the worst outbreak of anti-Semitism since World War II, many Jews have also discovered—painfully—that their Jewish identity is worth knowing and fighting for. I believe Jewish history teaches that our best protection from those who wish us harm comes from living with authentic Jewish faith, pride, and unity. That's why I believe that the horrors of October 7 have turned my story from what I hoped would be a valuable and entertaining memoir about building a meaningful life and career to something bigger: a wake-up call to Jewish pride, a refusal to live in fear, and a pathway to that meaningful, professionally fulfilling life. A Jewish awakening has come at a terrible price.

Jewish teachings have inspired my professional ambitions and personal values. They have helped me build an empowering spiritual life and taught me to make my words count for the good. I will always continue to stand up proudly as a Jew even during dark times.

Because a brighter tomorrow is sure to come.

Young, Fearless, and Foolish

You are smart, smart, smart—but you are not so smart!
—Yiddish proverb

I learned my first hard-won lesson about the world of journalism at age eighteen, a college freshman hell-bent on a writing career. I had offered to write a short feature for the UCLA Jewish student paper, *Ha'Am* ("the nation"), and was elated when the editor gave me the go-ahead.

I raced through the next edition of the paper to find my story. There it was—my first byline! I tingled with excitement. But as my eyes danced across the first lines of the article, I realized it had been almost completely rewritten. Why had the editor taken a hatchet to my maiden journalistic gem? In self-righteous pique, I barged into the newspaper's office and lashed out at the editor. If my article had been so bad, why didn't she give me a chance to make it right, or at least remove my name from a story that was no longer mine?

The editor defended herself, pointing out my total inexperience in journalism as well as her need to get the paper to the printer quickly. When I harrumphed that I would never write for her again, it's a wonder she didn't jump out of her seat and shout, "Thank God!"

Growing up, I had been generously praised by my parents, grandparents, and teachers for my facility with language. Believing my own good press gave me an extravagant sense of my own abilities. This was my first reality check about my writing and one of many crucial lessons that would serve to humble me along my road to becoming the best writer I could be.

From early childhood, books were magical wonderlands. When I was five, I lay in bed with rapt attention as my father read to me from *The Wizard of Oz*, though to my consternation he frequently fell asleep in the middle of the chapter. When I was seven, I was absorbed by *The Five Little Peppers and How They Grew, Charlotte's Web,* and other classics. My insatiable appetite to absorb the written word wasn't always beneficial. In the late 1960s, I read both *Time* and *Newsweek*, filling my mind with nerve-racking knowledge about war, violent protests, drug overdoses, and assassinations. This was a heavy psychological load that made my world feel scary and unstable.

Still, there was no help from my reading addiction. I excelled in all my English classes as emphatically as I flailed in every math and science class. With these lopsided abilities, I banked on my language skills to propel me forward into a writing career. Despite my first journalistic flop, in the spring of my sophomore year I won a summer journalism internship in New York with the Jewish Student Press Service. Only one intern was chosen each summer, and my stories would get picked up by subscribing Jewish newspapers across the country.

Journalism skills were only part of my fabulous education that summer. I was no urban sophisticate, having grown up in Van Nuys, one of several sleepy suburbs in the San Fernando Valley. In Manhattan I felt like a hick, and in the heat of the summer, a sticky one at that. I had heard about this barometric condition called "humidity" that existed in New York. But as a native Angeleno, I'd only read about it in books or seen actors sweating from it in movies. Walking the steamy streets in July and August and descending into the clammy, smelly subway platforms below, I learned the meaning of the word. The air conditioning on the F train I took each day from Brooklyn to Manhattan only seemed to work a few days a week. Grasping the metal ring that hung from the ceiling of the subway car, I tried not to fall directly into the malodorous armpit of the man holding onto the ring next to me as we hurtled forward together.

My light, cool cotton shirts from the Indian boutiques in lower Manhattan were all getting ruined from sweat.

In addition to learning to survive the heat and sweat of subway rides, I also learned first-hand about three-card monte. Walking up Lexington one afternoon, I stopped to watch young toughs in jeans and T-shirts holding court on their "desks" of overturned boxes. My eyes popped open wide watching a customer guess the right playing card, magically turning his twenty-dollar bill into two twenties. It looked so easy! I had never seen any game like this before. As a student hard up for cash and earning a pittance for my internship, before I knew it I was handing over one twenty, then two, both of which were stuffed into the jeans pocket of one of the young sharks after I guessed the wrong card.

My sudden loss of forty dollars cut deeply—it was food money for the better part of a week. I had fallen for the con, and I was angry at myself for being a rube, but I was angrier still at the duplicitous duo plying their trade. They wore hard expressions, but I brazenly sidled next to one of them and murmured that I would not leave until he gave me my money back.

He ignored me. I didn't move. He pocketed another hundred bucks or so from other dupes and then I repeated my demand. Wouldn't he be glad to get rid of me for the bargain price of forty dollars?

"If you don't give me back my money, I'm calling the police," I said *sotto voce*. I was drawing attention from a few bystanders, some of them with alarmed expressions, cueing me that I was probably out of my mind to be testing guys like this. The "proprietor" raised his voice and said, "Lady, you call the police and we both go to jail, because you just gambled and gambling's illegal in New Yawk!"

Who knew? Not me!

My student poverty and outrage overrode my common sense. "I'm not leaving till I get my money," I repeated. No sooner had the words left my mouth than panic flooded my body. I had gone past the tipping point. Was I actually risking my life for forty bucks?

Apparently, yes! Suddenly, he reached into his pocket and slammed two crumbled twenty-dollar bills into my hand. "Get *outta heah*," he growled.

I bolted up the avenue. My heart pounded so hard that I put my hand over my heart to try to keep that vital organ from leaping out and in search of a saner home. I hid out in various stores, unable to calm down. I stole glances to see if anyone was coming after me. A half hour later, burrowing in a basement-level bookstore, I felt calmer. What could be safer than a bookstore? Maybe they'd let me stay the night, and I'd clutch a copy of *Pride and Prejudice*, dreaming of Pemberley. Just as I considered the ordeal truly over and my breathing rate had returned to normal, a very tall, extremely muscular man approached me and said, "Hey, that was you playing three-card monte down the street, wasn't it?"

Had he been following me? If so, how had I missed such a hulking presence? His sudden appearance and question terrified me so much I thought I would collapse on the spot.

"Yes . . ." I managed to whisper.

"You oughta be careful out there," he cautioned, shaking his head in disapproval. "Those guys were watching you. Don't ever do that again."

"I won't, I promise. I won't ever play any card game anywhere in the Tri-State area, or even in the known universe," I vowed, trembling. He left, and I stayed in the Classics aisle until closing time. On the way to the subway, I found a pay phone to call my housemates in Brooklyn, native New Yorkers who were renting me a room. They expressed shock at my antics and warned me to watch my back as I made my way underground to the train.

A few weeks later I found myself lost in the Bowery at dusk. I had made plans to have dinner with Ben, a good friend and fellow English major from UCLA. He gave me directions to his loft apartment involving a train, a bus, and then a brief walk. The bus trundled through neighborhoods that were getting sketchier and grimier and with a higher per capita ratio of drunks with every block. I clearly had missed the stop and nervously exited the bus in a neighborhood with few people capable of standing upright or seeming to be sentient, so I sought help in a tiny bodega.

Five tough-looking guys faced me from behind and in front of the small counter. Forbidding musculature was on display through their tight T-shirts. I was young, female, and alone. My sense of vulnerability to attack was fully engaged, honed by thousands of years of persecution against Jews and by New York's high crime rate. Frequent headlines in the tabloids splashed photos of the latest victims of criminal assaults, many of them young women. I began to understand why New York was called the city that never sleeps. With dangerous villains lurking all around, who could sleep?

I stood stock still, paralyzed with a level of terror that made my fear after escaping from three-card monte seem like bush league. My mind went blank. I could not utter a single syllable as I stared at the guys, and they stared right back. I couldn't remember my friend's name. (It was Ben.) I couldn't remember the name of his street. (It was Houston.) I couldn't even remember my own name. (It was Judy.) I thought of my parents, who loved me so much and who might never see me again.

While most of my brain synapses were misfiring, I did register the fact that none of these young men with powerful muscles had made any move to violate any part of my person. This was cheering. Finally, one of the guys asked, "Whaddaya want?"

I stammered and stuttered, my entire body quaking. In a barely audible voice I asked how to get to the address on Houston Street. I saw pity in their eyes. One of them walked me outside and in his heavily accented English directed me where to turn left, then right, to find my friend's apartment.

They weren't going to kill me! I would see my parents again! I still had a future in journalism! Frankly, I hadn't learned much journalism yet, but I was becoming street savvier by the moment. "Thank you! Thank you!" I groveled, after being given directions.

As I focused on following the directions, I realized that I had an uncanny knack for making people very happy by just agreeing to go away: the editor of the UCLA Jewish student paper. The three-card monte dealer. The guys in the bodega. Perhaps this was something I needed to work on.

An hour late, I rode up the old, creaky elevator in the converted warehouse to Ben's fourth-floor loft, falling into his arms and blabbering dramatically about my near miss with becoming another crime statistic in New York. After dinner Ben seemed glad to get rid of me, too.

I learned that surviving in New York required rules. Rule one: no card games on the street, especially when the playing field is an upside-down cardboard box. Rule two: make sure you have explicit directions when seeking an unfamiliar address. Rule three: choose a theme song to sing during scary moments. That summer, I chose the Bee Gees' "Stayin Alive."

Still, New York was a fabulous place to spend my summer. I chomped on the biggest, chewiest bagels my teeth had ever met and the likes of which had not yet traveled as far west as Los Angeles. I discovered Entenmann's cakes and donuts, similarly foreign, tantalizing, and addicting. Most crucially, I began to earn my chops as a reporter. My editor, Eli, sent me all over the city to interview Jews who were innovators in the world of arts, culture, and religion. Following two opposing trends, I covered both the emergence of gay synagogues on one hand and the rising trend of nonreligious Jews becoming Orthodox on the other, interviewing participants in both movements. I loved asking people questions that would otherwise have been none of my business. My interest was genuine, which earned trust, so interviewees talked openly about their experiences, innovations, and perspectives. At the time I wasn't shopping for a deeper religious experience or affiliation. I did not observe Shabbat, but I also did not eat nonkosher meat. Judaism was my identity, emotionally and culturally.

I was elated to see my stories getting published in subscribing newspapers in many states, but that ego boost was tempered by realizing how much I had to learn about good feature writing. When Eli sat me down to review his edits on the first story I turned in, my heart sank as I saw my copy hemorrhaging red ink. My face must have registered the shock because Eli said, "Look, Judy. If you want to be a professional writer, you can never be jealous of your own words."

I got the message. My words were hardly sacred, and in many cases they may not even have been appropriate, specific, or well-chosen. More than almost anything else in the world, I wanted to be an outstanding writer, and Eli was an outstanding teacher. He was an accomplished, smart editor, toiling in a low-paying field for the greater good of helping to train future journalists in Jewish media. Whatever Eli told me to do, I would do.

He patiently showed me my mistakes. Passive voice. Mixed tenses. Places where I should have asked a follow-up question but didn't. Places where I had written too much. Or too little. I saw and understood. I would staunch the flow of red ink on my next assignments. I would show him that I could write.

With Ink-Stained Hands

What a newspaper needs in its news, in its headlines, and on its editorial page is terseness, humor, descriptive power, satire, originality, good literary style, clever condensation, and accuracy, accuracy, accuracy!
—Joseph Pulitzer

Eli's edits were considerably lighter on my final stories, and we were both satisfied that nearly all my pieces were being published in subscribing newspapers throughout North America. At the end of the internship, Eli invited me to become a student member of the board of directors of the press service. That would have been triumph enough for me in the summer of 1980, but the icing on the cake was discovering an opening with the staff of the Jewish quarterly newspaper at UC Berkeley, where I would transfer for my junior year.

I had visited Berkeley the previous spring to visit my friend Miriam. I was enchanted by the beauty of the Bay Area and enticed by a vision of living outside of LA for the first time. As Miriam saw me gazing out of her big bay window at the clear blue skies and leafy trees swaying in the breeze, she suggested, "Why don't you transfer?" I'd fit in perfectly at Berkeley with my Birkenstocks, commitment to recycling, and willingness to eat Miriam's baked tofu and miso soup. Expanding my vistas academically and geographically seemed like a smart move.

Miriam and I shared a house on Parker Street with two other women. We were nestled between a Seventh-Day Adventist church and another California bungalow-style house where an Irish expat couple lived with their two young children. The husband, Patrick, was an old-school bookbinder with a basement-level studio. I loved watching him working at his craft, carefully turning the handles of an iron nipping press in a corkscrew fashion and pressing the metal plate to secure the leather-tooled cover of the book he was creating. In his eyes I saw intense focus on his workmanship and the pleasure of creativity.

Unlike the trendy college neighborhood of Westwood, Berkeley resolutely and proudly maintained its 1960s persona, from the dimly lit, slightly shabby coffee houses and popular T-shirts emblazoned with the town's nickname, "Bezerkeley" to the hippie holdovers for whom time had stopped around 1966. These included the graying, diminutive woman known as the "dog lady" who walked up and down Telegraph Avenue every day with five chihuahuas poking their tiny faces out from numerous pockets of her strange, discolored vest; the "orange man" who stood frozen outside the main entrance of campus, holding oranges in each hand; and a cast of other psychedelic characters. Some antidrug literature might have gone a long way if they had only gotten to these folks in time.

My friend Ben had already transferred from UCLA, where we had taken a few of the same English lit classes together. Among my happiest memories from my two years there were when Ben and I read Shakespeare to each other in the living room of the Westwood Bayit, a Jewish student co-op where we both lived. Ben had a longtime girlfriend whom he adored, which may—or may not—explain why he failed to notice that I had a crush on him.

When I arrived at Berkeley and learned that Ben was the new editor of Berkeley's Jewish student paper, *Ha'Etgar* ("The Challenge"), I decided that I wanted more from him than the mere friendship he'd offered me so far. The position of girlfriend was taken, but the position of Ben's assistant editor was wide open. He hadn't advertised the need for any help, but that didn't stop me from bolting up the two flights of stairs to the newspaper's minuscule office in the student union building, where I found Ben at a desk, mapping out the content of the first issue.

"Hi! What brings you here?" he asked.

"I'm your new assistant editor!" I announced. Ben wasn't bothered at all by my chutzpah. He just broadly threw his arms open wide and said, "Great! Let's get to work!"

I told Ben I'd do whatever he needed me to do, which turned out to be helping on just about every journalistic front: selling advertising, recruiting writers, drafting fundraising ads begging readers for donations to keep our humble enterprise afloat, editing articles, proofing all the typeset copy, and physically laying out every inch of text, artwork, and ads on large worktables in a printer's studio in a sketchy area of Oakland. I developed a good eye and a steady hand, which was helpful when overlaying single lines of corrected type that had errors and were only one-sixteenth of an inch high.

We published features about Jewish life—not only locally but internationally, including an update on the plight of Soviet Jewry and a feature highlighting four Berkeley alumni who explained their decision to make *Aliyah*, or move to Israel. We solicited a smattering of book reviews, poetry, short fiction, essays, and interviews with artists and other interesting folks and published a calendar of community events.

At my suggestion, Ben allowed a regular feature on Yiddish, which I was taking as a foreign language. My professor, Dr. Leonard Talmy, joked that its placement in the German department might have been a form of reparations. The column, "A Bisl Yiddish," introduced readers to some of the robust curses and slanders for which Yiddish is famous, including the much-beloved *Er zol vaksen vi a tsibeleh, mit dem kop in drerd!* ("May you grow like an onion with your head in the ground"), and, in a column devoted to expressions of exasperation, the vivid expression *Ikh nem de gederen!* ("I'm removing my viscera!") Yiddish was an endless fount of flamboyant deprecations, defamations, and other terms of abuse, including one of my favorites, *A mise-meshune zol im khapn!* ("May an unnatural death seize him!"), one that I envisioned when thinking about the evildoers who still abounded in the world. Professor Talmy also explained how to substitute the word for woman, *ir*, for the male pronoun *im* or *zayn*, because Yiddish is an equal opportunity vilifier of the worst in the human condition.

I covered a conference in San Francisco about anti-Semitism within the feminist movement and titled my story, "What's a Smart Feminist Like You Doing Wearing a Jewish Star?" This nasty question had been asked of several feminists, some of whom had responded by reaching toward greater Jewish practice. This is an old story. Historically, secular or relatively uninvolved Jews eventually discover that their apathy toward their faith is no defense against the relentless forces of anti-Semitism. But if you have to pay the price for being Jewish, why not at least explore the benefits and features?

I admired the overall goal of this gathering while being shocked by the many "separatists" in the crowd, women who refused to associate with men in any way. Butch haircuts, mannish mannerisms, and seething anger made the room feel hot, and I doubt there was a drop of nail polish within 100 miles of this event. When a man accidentally opened one of the doors to the hall where this confab was taking place, a woman screamed, "A MAN!" There were shouts as a few women began to chase him away, but he had run for his life.

It was tempting to include this wild episode in my write-up, and I wrestled with the decision, finally deciding to spare them the embarrassment. I judged it a greater good to point to the problem of anti-Semitism within the feminist movement rather than shine a light on the extremists in their ranks. I felt the weight of responsibility in making this call, the kind of judgment that journalists make every day. Our own agendas cannot help but color our work. Who do we quote, who do we ignore, or quote without appropriate context, shaping the truth as we wanted it to be shaped? What nasty little scenes, or beautiful little scenes, do we choose to include or ignore, "helping" readers draw the conclusions that we hope they will draw?

This conference gave me a chilling look at what happens when political philosophies have no guardrails, not stopping at their logical limits but rushing headlong into extremism. Even the nonseparatists radiated a blanket hostility to men that was obnoxious and inhumane. I lost respect for the type of feminism I saw up in the Bay Area, so much so that I seriously considered letting my own very short hair grow long and losing the Birkenstocks.

Strident political opinions seemed to be the organic mother's milk of the entire Berkeley-San Francisco area, and we Jewish students were made to feel it on campus. For example, the Jewish Student Union's table on Sproul Plaza was set up across the way from the table of the pro-Arab student group. I hung out at the JSU table with my friends, many of whom were active in other Jewish student groups. The anger and enmity that some among the pro-Arab group directed toward us was palpable and frightening. Their banners and flyers heatedly and blindly criticized Israel as an "apartheid" and illegitimate state. This calumny had its roots in Cold War-era Soviet rhetoric and led to the term "Zionist" becoming a thinly veiled cover for the word "Jew." In 1975, the Soviet Union and most Arab states added to the majority who voted to pass resolution 3379 in the UN General Assembly, equating Zionism with racism. That poisonous lie had festered for years and unfortunately, infected many students, who believed that Israel was the true oppressor of the Palestinians, refusing to acknowledge the continuous cycle of Arab attacks on the State of Israel from the moment of its inception.

The situation was both scary and sad. I had visited Israel twice, first when I was thirteen and my mother and maternal grandparents took me there as a bat mitzvah gift. The second time, I was sixteen and spent a glorious summer with a large group of high school students, working on a kibbutz and traveling throughout the tiny country. As so many other Jews have experienced—often to their surprise—stepping onto the ground in Israel awakened something inside my soul, an intangible, startling, powerful sense that I was home. Anti-semitism on campus and wherever it flared in the world only furthered my commitment to my Jewish identity. This commitment was also fueled by outrageous lies about Israel's treatment of Palestinians, the denial of Jewish roots in the land, and the bitterness of seeing and hearing media reports where Israelis were always the aggressor, while ignoring the flagrant and consistent violence by Palestinians and other Arabs against Jewish citizens, including women and children. Their school texts showed maps of the Middle East where Israel didn't exist and used vicious images and smears about Jews straight from Hitler's own propaganda machine. As an antidote, I would devote a great deal of my career to writing about my people, my religion, and my homeland.

After weeks of work on the paper, we spent a long night at the printer's studio, where Ben and I and a few other students we had roped into the task, physically laid out the newspaper, column by column. We stood there for hours, frequently asking the typesetter to reset lines of type where we found errors. Single lines of corrected type were only one-eighth of an inch wide, and it took almost surgical precision to lay it over typo-ridden lines evenly. This was a visually and physically demanding job, but I loved every minute of it.

Ben and I were gleeful when we went to pick up the five thousand copies of our paper at a huge printing plant in San Francisco in a station wagon requisitioned from the university. Ben parked at the mouth of the cavernous facility and we both leaped out, dashing breathlessly toward the massive piles of various print jobs, all stacked and securely held together with thick plastic bands. I loved the heady smell of fresh newsprint and ink and inhaled deeply. To me at that moment, it even smelled better than fresh-brewed coffee.

Although we faced a veritable sea of stacked, banded piles of magazines and newspapers in the giant facility, we instantly spied our "baby" and its black-and-white woodblock print of Natan (then

Anatoly) Sharansky on the cover. We rushed over and asked one of the employees to cut the cord. He neatly sliced the plastic on one of our stacks and we each grabbed a copy, examining our newborn with pride and perhaps a bit of astonishment.

We turned the pages rapidly, marveling at all sixteen pages of our handiwork. Despite all our efforts, it was still an amateur production. A few sentences here and there had been unceremoniously severed mid-line during the bleary-eyed hours of the final layout. Headline fonts we had chosen for their variety just looked arbitrary and mismatched in published form. Some text lines had been laid askew, looking slightly inebriated. But this was no time for self-flagellation. This was a time for two Jews to kvell in exultation.

We hugged. We had done it—we had made a newspaper.

After loading our five thousand newspapers into the wagon, the poor vehicle now sagged precariously on the steep, nearly vertical streets of downtown San Francisco. We lightened our load as quickly as we could, delivering copies at bookstores, coffee houses, the Hillel house, and throughout campus. With ink-stained hands we eagerly waited for praise from our readership and then began work on the next issue.

Ben and I were well-connected with the other Jewish students who were also energetically involved with Jewish life on campus and beyond. Each of our enterprises did take a village, and we all helped one another. One night at the Hillel House, a tall, pretty brunette smiled at me, gently grasped my arm, and asked if I would help her with a project she was organizing for the United Jewish Appeal. "Sure!" I said, immediately asking her, "And will you help me with the newspaper?" We both laughed, and Marcia and I became instant best friends.

Ben would graduate in June, but I had another year to go at Cal, perfectly positioned to slide into his role as managing editor of the paper. I had many changes planned, including a redesign of the logo and layout, and an expansion of pages if I could sell enough ads. Ben had modestly called himself "managing editor" in the masthead, without even using capital letters. Lacking his modesty, I would be "Editor in Chief," with capital letters.

Back in Los Angeles for a visit the following fall, I went to synagogue with my maternal grandfather, Papa Cohen, during the holiday of Sukkot. After the service everyone went outside to the large sukkah for the kiddush and refreshments. Papa was a well-connected local rabbi and was happily schmoozing with friends and acquaintances while I chatted with someone at the other end of the sukkah. Suddenly, in an act that I found profoundly out of character, Papa appeared at my side, placed a hand on my back, and steered me decisively away from my conversation and toward the other end of the booth. We practically barreled through the crowd, trying not to knock people's cookies or cups of tea out of their hands as we passed.

Papa parked me in front of another elderly man and said in his pronounced Polish accent, "Aaron! This is my granddaughter. She is the editor of the Jewish newspaper at the university at Berkeley!" The depth of pride in his voice just about brought me to tears. I understood my special status in his eyes. Papa loved all his grandchildren, of course, but I was the only one of them who was enthusiastic about living a Jewish life. Understandably, he may have viewed me as the only one of his descendants likely to carry on his religious legacy.

My role as editor of this little college publication resonated with Papa personally and professionally. In addition to working as a pulpit rabbi, teacher, and part-time rabbinic judge, Papa wrote voluminously and in erudite style for the Jewish press about Jewish education, philanthropy, issues surrounding aging, and profiles of dozens of Jewish writers. His doctoral dissertation in sociology was published as a book exploring the influence of American Jewish literature on American culture. If I had been born with the writing gene whose engine ran at full throttle, I surely had Papa Cohen to thank for it. It gratified me to know that the work that suffused me with creative energy and purpose also provided comfort to my eighty-two-year-old grandfather in his twilight years.

At the beginning of my senior year, I posted notices at school to recruit volunteer writers and a graphic artists. My helpers included Elizabeth, a short, barrel-shaped woman who made a startling appearance dressed head to toe in all black, Goth-style. She had phenomenal talent, and as a Gentile, she seemed delighted to have the opportunity to create illustrations for a Jewish publication. A serious-minded sophomore named Laura became my assistant editor, taking up where I had left off the previous year, selling ads, writing articles, editing copy, and rolling up her sleeves when it was time to lay out the paper at the printer's studio.

I was thrilled to be at the helm of the paper and part of the Jewish campus leadership. I surreptitiously edited articles during a boring government class. (I would pay for this later by failing the final exam.) Filling each issue with what I hoped was substantial, engaging content satisfied me creatively and intellectually.

In the second edition of the paper, I wrote an essay expressing sadness over an article I'd read in a local paper by a Jew who had struggled to find meaning in his religion yet found nothing positive to hold on to. I wrote:

> Judaism is a framework for my life. Far from being a series of limitations and restrictions, as some would think, it gives me freedom to develop myself as fully as possible, while reminding me of my humanity. Judaism tells me that I am only human, that I need constant improvement, but that my life is precious and that my life should be holy.
>
> It is impossible to fully convey how I feel about my Jewish identity in a few paragraphs. For me, there is a lot more to being Jewish than a history of martyrdom and grief, of prohibitions and guilt. Judaism is a celebration of life and a refusal to take anything we have in life for granted. Judaism maintains an ideal of infusing the highest possible degree of sanctity into one's life and relationships.

I wrote all this, despite the fact that I observed almost no rituals, did not observe Shabbat, and wasn't involved in ongoing Jewish studies other than my Yiddish language class. Very few of my actions seemed to back up my statements, but my limited Jewish education had still managed to convey fundamentally important Jewish concepts in broad strokes. These lessons had embedded themselves deep in the heart.

In my senior year I took a course in rhetoric, which taught classical methods and rigors involved in the art of persuasion. It is a discipline that has existed since biblical times, and Greeks and Romans used it with exquisite impact in their literature. I regretted that it was too late to change my major because I was enraptured by rhetoric. Papers written for English lit required me to analyze the symbolism of colors or names in *The Scarlet Letter* or to compare and contrast characters in Hardy, Shakespeare, or George Elliot. Rhetoric essays required me to craft cogent arguments using powerful rhetorical principles and devices that had vast possibilities.

Here's an example of *anaphora*, or repetition at the start:

> *He was goosed last night, he was goosed the night before last, he was goosed today. He has lately got in the way of being always goosed, and he can't stand it.* (Charles Dickens, *Hard Times*)

Here is a haunting example of *metanoia,* or correcting oneself:

> *But if this country cannot be saved without giving up that principle—I was about to say I would rather be assassinated on this spot than surrender it.* (Abraham Lincoln, address at Philadelphia, 1861)

Reversal of structure, or *chiasmus:*

> *People do not seem to talk for the sake of expressing their opinions, but to maintain an opinion for the sake of talking.* (William Hazlitt, "On Coffee-House Politicians," 1821)

What writer couldn't love all this? (By the way, these examples were not from my long-ago class, but from *Farnsworth's Classical English Rhetoric*, by Ward Farnsworth).

Learning the "Trades"

Creativity is allowing yourself to make mistakes. Art is knowing which ones to keep.
—Scott Adams

As graduation loomed, I began to worry about my job prospects as an English major with a little college journalism in the mix. Most of my friends planned to attend graduate school, *and* they had serious boyfriends to boot. From my first to final year of college, I expected a future husband to magically materialize and help solidify my future. But each year came and went and Mr. Right failed to show up. Where was he? At Berkeley, I dated a few men, including a funky, earthy backpacker; a successful entrepreneur who embarrassed me in front of my progressive comrades by picking me up for our date in a limousine; and a beautiful soul named Steven who was battling cancer. His strength, optimism, and religious faith moved me, and after he passed, I dedicated the following issue of the paper to his memory. Our student community suffered a shocking loss of a strapping and handsome student named Paul, who went trekking in Nepal and died after falling sick there. Life's fragility took our collective breath away.

As I considered my options, I understood that entry-level writing jobs were as low-paying as they were competitive. Assistant editors working in the "pink-collar ghetto" of New York's magazine publishing industry were a prime example, and I didn't want to start my grown-up life there. My best friend Marcia had moved to Israel, and I envied her gumption and commitment. I missed her so much, but she sounded happy in her letters.

Israel felt like the right move, yet I couldn't make such an enormous break with my family. My older brother, Allan, had died in a car accident years before and I needed to be near my parents, who had suffered the unthinkable in losing their only son. I could have gone to a small town, like Halfway, Oregon, and worked as a newspaper reporter, covering the controversial new traffic light on Main Street and the grand opening of The Chicken Shack, which offered homemade "Grizzly Garlic" and "Smokin' Sriracha" sauce for their chicken wings.

But neither the madness of Manhattan nor the hush of Halfway, Oregon sounded like they would suit me. Instead, I returned to Los Angeles, where I figured I'd certainly be able to find a writing job with one of the city's magazine publishers, organizations, or businesses. And maybe, somewhere in that city, I'd finally meet that elusive and handsome future husband, a Jewish mensch who would make Papa proud.

As a graduation gift, Papa Cohen paid for me to accompany my mother and Aunt Eleanor to the Soviet Union to visit my great-aunt Rosa and her family. Rosa was the only sister of Nana Cohen, my late grandmother, who had bravely sailed from her family and homeland at the age of sixteen. Nana would never have imagined when she originally departed Russia—all alone at age sixteen—that she wouldn't see her sister again for fifty-two years. She would never have imagined that her communication with her sister would be cut off for more than twenty years, a severing that began under Stalin and continued through Brezhnev's Communist rule. Nana worked like a gumshoe detective to track down anyone who could ferry their letters back and forth, and after years of effort she succeeded. In the mid-1960s, she found a letter smuggler, who helped the sisters resume communication. In 1974, when Nana was already in declining health, she made a solo trip back to Kyiv and shared a week-long, bittersweet reunion with her sister.

Before Nana died in 1977, she made my mother, Aunt Eleanor, and Papa promise to stay in close contact with Rosa and her family and go to the Soviet Union if possible. After such a painful and protracted cutting of the family bond, it meant the world to Nana to keep that bond despite a formidable language barrier. The three kept their promise, and in 1979 they flew to Kyiv to visit Rosa and her family. Mom and Aunt Eleanor practiced rudimentary Russian and brushed up on their Yiddish, which they could use to speak with Rosa—but only inside their tiny apartment. Now, three years later and with Rosa quite elderly, Mom and Eleanor were eager to go again, and thanks to my Papa's generosity, I was able to accompany them.

From the minute we landed, an atmosphere of oppression weighed thickly in the air. Never before had I experienced the feeling of being watched and mistrusted. Was it because I was an American? A Jew? Both? They knew we were Jewish, because we had to state the purpose of our trip and whom we would visit on our visa applications. At the airport, Mom and I were immediately and roughly hustled away from Eleanor to a separate room by a short, stocky, sour Svetlana who intimidated and bullied us, examining our belongings with bumbling and ludicrous attention. If she hadn't scared me, I would have laughed at her power-tripping performance. With an expression that suggested she was still working on digesting last week's kasha, she pawed through our suitcases, tossing everything onto a large white counter. She randomly turned articles of clothing inside out, unzipped every zipped compartment, and twisted open lipstick tubes. Did she really think we had hidden any minuscule contraband in there, or did she want to see the luscious mauves and pinks that smoothly glided over American lips when she had to stand in line for two days just to buy a dried-out tube of Russkie Red lipstick?

In fact, few of the clothes were ours. We had stuffed our suitcases with items specifically requested by our family: Levi's jeans and other quality, American-made shirts, pants, dresses, sweaters, and children's clothing. But we knew gifts were not allowed inside the Soviet Union—why allow anything into a country with a planned economy where queuing in line for toilet paper was practically a national sport? My heart pounded as she repeatedly asked in accusing tones, "These clothes are yours? Or are they *gifts?*" Mom and I lied, praying we wouldn't be hauled off to some remote version of the Pale of Settlement where my own ancestors had been trapped for generations.

I was a nervous wreck by the time we arrived at Aunt Rosa's apartment inside a squat, long, bleak apartment complex that appeared to have been designed to induce clinical depression. When she opened the door and I saw how much she looked like Nana, I fell into her plump arms with tears of joy and relief. We spent our days with Rosa and her daughter, Nella. Rosa's son, Viktor, worked in refrigeration. Because of his professional contacts, he was able to score fresh vegetables, chicken, and bakery goods that would otherwise have been unimaginable. We returned each night to our hotel room, which had clearly been searched while we were out. They wanted us to know that they were watching.

One day I asked Aunt Rosa something in Yiddish while we were on a public bus. Though my Yiddish was rudimentary, it was the only language we had in common. Rosa's eyes darted left and right in fear as she placed a finger to her lips and whispered to me, "*In der haym.*" In the house. I felt so foolish for my gaffe. Where did I think I was, Brooklyn? Here in the Soviet Union, one didn't advertise one's Jewishness in public.

My Aunt Rosa's visceral fear of anyone hearing us speak a language that would mark us as Jews became a touchstone moment for me on this trip. Yes, there was anti-Semitism in the United States, but we hardly needed to hide our religious identity on the street. We could wear Jewish star pendants, men could wear kippahs on their heads, and we could gather for festivals celebrating Israel's Independence Day in public parks. Far from persecuting us, our government protected us with police to ensure our security during such high-profile events.

After our week with family in Kyiv, I flew alone to Moscow and joined a tour group for another week. While in the capital, I wanted to go to Moscow's synagogue, where Natan Sharansky had gone to pray before being arrested and locked up for nine years, becoming an international symbol of the Jewish "refusenik" movement. When I asked for the address at my hotel, the desk clerk looked at me and said, "Why do you go there? Nobody is there." I repeated my request and hailed a taxi. I left the country with many incredible experiences and a much more profound appreciation for the freedom I took for granted at home in the United States, not least of which were freedom of movement, speech, and religion.

Back at home with my parents, I scoured the editorial or writer listings in the "Help Wanted" ads. I subscribed to writers' magazines and sent story pitches to major magazines in New York, crafting and typing each letter with scrupulous care, including the self-addressed stamped envelope that was de rigueur in those days. A month or so later, each of my SASEs would wend its way back to me with the magazine's standard rejection note enclosed, including the boilerplate copy wishing me luck with my future writing endeavors. I had yet to achieve my next professional goal of being published in a large-circulation secular newspaper or magazine, but I knew I'd break through one day.

On Tuesday nights, I began to frequent Café Dansa, a pocket-sized club on LA's West Side that offered Israeli dancing. I had plenty of time on my hands and plenty of energy to dance off. This became a highlight of my week. Most everyone was young, with a smattering of older adults who still had the moves. I admired how fit they stayed and made a note to myself: never stop dancing!

One night at Café Dansa I met a man named Stuart, an executive at Cedars-Sinai Hospital. Tall, slim, with curly dark hair and a gentle personality, he was also sixteen years my senior. I saw that he wanted to ask me out and was determined to politely decline when he did. However, when I mentioned my job hunt for a writing position, he offered to put me in touch with a friend of his, a magazine publisher who was looking to hire a full-time writer. I gave him my number so that he could pass her information along to me. My job search was going nowhere fast, so when he called to tell me that she was interested in meeting me, he also asked me out on a date. I said yes.

Within a week, I was dressed for success and presented myself to Stuart's publisher friend, Carol. She was launching a new magazine, but I had no idea what it was about. Carol was in her midforties and dressed in an expensive, refined style. Her perfectly manicured nails were painted mauve and her wavy, shoulder-length hair framed an attractive face expertly made up. Her smooth, dark wood desk was piled with stacks of paper and various file folders, a hub of publishing decision-making with Carol as its commander.

I sat ramrod straight in a chair across from her as she reviewed my resume, which I had printed on cream-colored linen paper stock. In a slightly raspy smoker's voice, Carol asked me several questions about my experiences in writing and reporting. I hoped I was making a good impression. It sure felt strange to interview for a writing job whose subject remained shrouded in mystery, but whatever it was, I wanted it. Carol's other magazines were in the healthcare field—one was for EMTs, another for specialists in dialysis and transplantation, so it would probably be something valuable and dramatic. While visions of ambulances and caring doctors, nurses, and EMTs still danced in my head, Carol set my resume and cover letter down and began to tell me about her new magazine, *Hospital Gift Shop Management*.

What had she just said? I couldn't have heard that right.

"Um, what sort of articles would there be?" I blurted out, assuming I had just killed this job prospect. Weren't hospital gift shops just like gas station shops, only with teddy bears, knitted newborn hats, and candy bars? But she was a shrewd businesswoman and began ticking off a bounty of article topics, tapping each one of her beautifully manicured fingers against their mates on her other hand as she listed them.

"There are management issues, since most hospital gift shops are run by volunteers, and it can be hard to keep a solid staff," she explained. "There are issues of how to display merchandise attractively in a small space, dealing with shoplifting, and lots of other concerns of a retail establishment."

I nodded my head, understanding slowly dawning. Why shouldn't this itty-bitty niche in the retail world have its own magazine? And why shouldn't I become its national reporter? I liked Carol and I got the feeling that she liked me, too. I could have been her daughter, a daughter following in her own publishing footsteps. Carol not only offered me the job but at a salary several thousand dollars more a year than I had hoped to get. (Seeing the consistently pathetic wages offered for starting writing jobs had trained me to expect third-world wages.) I rushed home in excitement, hugging my mother and father over my new employment status. I was a writer! A paid, full-time writer!

On my first day at work, Carol took me out to a fine restaurant for lunch, just the two of us. I listened with great interest as she told me about how she and her copublisher, Debbie, had launched the company together as divorced, single mothers who needed to earn a living. With a staff of more than thirty employees, Creative Age Publishing produced four magazines (which we called "books"), all fat with advertising—the name of the game. I felt blessed with good fortune that my new boss meant to take me under her wing.

Having a regular job from 8:30 a.m. to 4:30 p.m. and a half hour for lunch presented a paradigm shift in my life. I had no homework. I retired my resume. Most of my friends from high school and college were attending grad school in other cities, and my social life crawled to a near halt. For the first time in my sheltered life, I was also in "the real world," working with a colorful crew of office colleagues. Debbie often swore a blue streak and pounded the hallways in her high heels, shrilly fuming about the electricity bill or a canceled ad contract. Her gripes made the rest of us laugh, since she and Carol had their manicurists make house calls to the office each Wednesday, and they spent lavishly on travel and dining. (My own expensed lunch with Carol, on the other hand, was clearly a vital company expense.)

Jeanne, proofreader extraordinaire, retained her eagle-eyed attention to detail even in the bathroom. Short, middle-aged, and with a slight lisp, Jeanne must have taken note of all the women's shoes each morning as we filed into our offices. How else to explain, during what should have been my private moments, Jeanne calling from the next stall, "Is that you, Judy?" I became especially friendly with our two lively graphic designers, Chris and Donna, both from the Midwest.

I continued to date Stuart, and my parents, bless their hearts, said not one word about the considerable age difference between us. "He's a nice boy," my sweet father said about my thirty-eight-year-old boyfriend. Stuart *was* "a nice boy," but not for me. He had entered my life at the right time, to be an emissary of sorts between unemployment and my first real job. However, I became increasingly uncomfortable with our age difference and ended it.

Working for "the trades," the world of industry-specific magazines, led to a certain social awkwardness. Trade magazines included prestigious titles such as *Editor & Publisher* and *Variety,* but the vast majority were far down the food chain and included titles such as *Candy Nut & Wholesaler; Chickens—The Essential Poultry Publication;* or, in my case, *Hospital Gift Shop Management.* Answering the question, "And what do *you* do?" at parties always caused me to suck in my breath before I answered. Uttering the name of my magazine usually led to blank stares and a moment later, a sudden recollection by my conversation partner of an urgent phone call that needed to be made.

At twenty-two years old, I was young and inexperienced in most of the ways of the world, including business. My parents' friends were teachers, accountants, legal secretaries, or technicians. I heard no stories about the demands and issues involved in the daily operations of running a business of any size. I had held part-time jobs from the time I was fifteen, first at a stationery and gift store and then at an Arby's fast-food joint in a dodgy area of Van Nuys. I rode my bike the two miles there and back from our house. Working that job exposed me to many people living at life's roughest edges. It made me especially sad to see the looks of resignation in the eyes of the young women wearing too much cheap eye shadow and micro-miniskirts, who came in with a different man each night. One night, after a rare double shift, I burned my fingers while cleaning the fryer, searing two of them together. But every cloud has a silver lining, and I was only too happy to keep returning to the hospital clinic three times a week, literally offering my left hand to the handsome interns who gently changed my dressings.

Writing for *Hospital Gift Shop Management* proved surprisingly satisfying. I wanted my work to be meaningful in some way, and all of us who worked on the magazine quickly grew fond of our primary readership—the mostly middle-aged and even elderly "blue-haired" ladies who usually ran those operations, often as volunteers. They were in it heart and soul for the benefit of the hospital. We treated their mission with respect, serving up authoritative advice and sophisticated ideas geared toward their niche market.

Carol impressed me with her bountiful story ideas and my docket was full, writing about strategies for working with hospital administrators, best practices in recruiting and retaining a volunteer staff, advice from security experts on preventing shoplifting, and the latest gift trend ideas.

One day the managing editor, Barbara, chose one of our stockpiled management columns, written by various guest authors, for the upcoming issue. "Better call this guy's office and make sure he's not dead. We've had this one for six months," she said in her usual flippant style, handing me the copy from her desk opposite mine. I just laughed and shook my head, but I began dialing. When I asked to speak to Mr. Barton, there was a shocked silence of several seconds.

"I'm sorry to tell you that Mr. Barton passed away in March," the secretary told me sadly.

"He really is dead," I told Barbara after I hung up the phone, incredulous. "I can't believe it!"

"Told you we needed to call," she shrugged. "Always make sure guest authors still have a pulse by the time you run the story." Barbara was a good editor, but the sympathy gene in her family may have skipped a generation.

My work was respectable trade industry journalism, though still lightweight. I didn't need a flak jacket or have to smuggle myself in the back of a truck and tunnel under a burlap sack in order to interview a gift shop manager in Missoula, Montana about her most surprising top-selling gifts for men during the holiday season. I had given a great deal of thought about the kind of journalism I wanted to practice during my lifetime, and although I followed politics very closely, I couldn't picture myself performing acts of great journalistic bravery and reporting from danger zones—urban or foreign. I had enormous respect for journalists who waded into troubled regions and did the heavy lifting there. Hundreds have died while covering war-torn and other perilous places and they deserve our respect and appreciation. I was brave, but not that brave.

At this early stage I was still a scrapper, working in the safe and cushy world of trade magazines. Still my job at Creative Age Publishing provided invaluable daily practice in reporting and writing. Our readership was small but appreciative, and I loved hearing the delight in the voices of surprised hospital gift shop managers or industry experts when I cold-called and asked for interviews. Nobody ever refused—the stories gave them great PR. No exposés in *HGSM* about a Volunteer of the Month extorting from the COO or trafficking in black market baby blankets to be sold in the gift shops.

I fell in love with people in the South, their authentic kindness spoken in a honey-soaked drawl. Midwesterners were warm and friendly, and I even began to detect the subtle difference between an Illinois accent and one from Wisconsin. Some assignments were almost too fun to be considered work. At the gift show at Los

Angeles's massive convention center, I walked miles of aisles for a story on gift trends for Christmas, loading swag into my promo bag and sampling edible treats. I became a sophisticate in discerning quality plush toys (I no longer called them stuffed animals), and just a few days after a boyfriend dumped me, I followed the motto of one of our advertisers, "Gotta Get a Gund," and bought Harold, a tan, foot-high teddy bear with sincere black eyes. He was my therapy teddy bear.

It wasn't only my knowledge of retailing that expanded. I began to appreciate and take pride in our country's devotion to voluntarism. It was a beautiful thing, and I doubted that most other countries could equal America's volunteer spirit. My work also softened my built-in mistrust of the business world. Hollywood films and TV shows often portrayed business bosses as heartless men who cared only for money and employees as victims of their Dickensian greed. But while I wrote about philanthropic little businesses, my eyes were opened to the real-world challenges facing anyone managing a for-profit operation. These included training and maintaining a stable staff, dealing with difficult customers, responding to ever-changing market conditions, controlling inventory, and managing vendor relationships, among other things.

This didn't stop my friends and me from laughing at our own bosses and their love of luxury. They drove shiny new Mercedes automobiles that our work helped pay for, while most of us drove older cars with faded paint that frequently needed repairs. We groused about the grim-faced bookkeeper who docked us for even a single minute we clocked in late or took an extra five minutes for lunch.

And before the chiefs sailed off for a holiday vacation on a sun-drenched island sipping daiquiris, we rolled our eyes at what felt were miserly holiday gifts. One year, they presented us with boxed sets of dried meats and cheeses, handing them to us with beatific expressions that suggested they could hardly believe their own generosity. I instantly regifted my *treyf* holiday gift to my friends, feeling cheated of any tangible appreciation for my contributions.

Still, this job was a huge gift. It was rare to score a full-time writing job right out of college, and I appreciated Carol's ongoing tutelage. Her writing reflected her fashion sense: stylish and smart, never overdone, setting just the right tone. And I knew that her mentoring was a vote of confidence, worth more than any holiday bonus.

One day I asked Carol to let me edit a short piece for one of the medical magazines and she obliged me. I turned it in, feeling unnaturally proud of myself. The next day, she took the very unusual step of walking from her executive office down the hallway to our little editorial lair. She poked her head inside the office I shared with Barbara and beckoned me: "Judy, please come to my office."

This couldn't be good. I followed Carol back to her command center, nerves jangling, while admiring her day's ensemble of a peach silk blouse, tailored gray pants, and designer heels. Seated across the divide of her imposing, titanic desk, I waited for Carol to speak.

"Judy, you're a good writer, but you'll never be an editor." Her words detonated, leaving my ego a pile of rubble. My mouth was parched as Carol then enumerated the many ways I had missed opportunities to clean up and refine the article I had edited. I paid attention to everything she said, wanting to learn, but her unexpected criticism stung badly. I also felt angry and confused. So far, she had been consistently complimentary about my progress. It made no sense to me that someone who could write capably could *never* become an editor. Never is a long time!

I believed that a good writer nurtures her love and respect for the written word and understands the ingredients of prose that flows logically and at times, lyrically. A good writer is committed to the practice of writing as an art and a craft. I believed an understanding of the "elements of style" that comprise effective, articulate, affecting writing was a completely transferable skill to the craft of editing. Perhaps this wasn't necessarily true for all other writers, but I felt a fiery determination that it would be true for me.

Carol was my employer and my mentor, but I would prove her wrong.

A few weeks after this meeting, I asked Carol to let me try editing again. In the interim, I had scrutinized my writing with greater care, remembering the lessons she taught me during what had been a sobering tutorial. This time, she was pleased with the results, and a few months later she promoted me from staff writer to assistant editor.

Hard-Won Lessons in Humor Writing

When humor goes, there goes civilization.
—Erma Bombeck

One Saturday evening as the sun nestled down toward the horizon, I popped a quarter into the newspaper vending machine on Main Street in Venice to grab the *Los Angeles Herald-Examiner*. I dumped the inner feature sections in the trash can and snapped open the main news section to the last page, my eyes greedily scanning the letters to the editor. The week before, the paper had run my humor essay—my first sale to a major newspaper—titled, "Fear of Fat: Don't Let it Make You Skinny," and I had hoped to see a letter praising its brilliance and hilarity.

This is how my essay in the "Saturday Story" feature began:

> Last Wednesday afternoon at 4:30, I was peacefully braising in the sauna of one of the local health clubs, now as common a fixture on our landscape as the golden arches. I had just toiled through another jazzercize class, led by a willowy, taut, and polished young woman dressed in a slick, expensive exercise outfit. I relaxed on the hot bench, feeling proud of myself for having exercised, trying to calculate how many calories I had burned up so far that day. Suddenly, the only other woman in the sauna—a perfect stranger—sat up and

said, "Potatoes are fattening, aren't they?" in a tone suggesting that she had been stricken by some terrible revelation.

The piece skewered the self-sabotaging habits of many women (including me) who did absurd things, such as order a slab of chocolate fudge cake at a restaurant but make sure they used sugar substitute when their coffee was served. We tortured ourselves at the gym, never satisfied with the bodies that worked so hard for us, day in and day out. Decades before the idea of "body positivity" became a "thing," it was a call for body positivity.

I knew that letters to the editor in response to the Saturday Story usually ran the following Saturday, which explains my near frenzy to find a letter applauding my work. You'd think I'd been completely unloved as a child given this bloated need for affirmation from complete strangers. But as I stood outside with my date, Rob, I scanned my name in one letter to the editor, my eyes bugging out and my jaw falling open in a socially awkward manner. The letter writer, a nabob from the American Diabetes Association, scorched me for my irresponsible attitude toward the nation's obesity epidemic. What kind of heartless individual joked about eating pumpkin pie or a Mr. Goodbar when at this very moment, somewhere in the nation a diabetic was having an insulin surge that could land her in the hospital?

I had been deliriously happy two weeks earlier when the editor of the Saturday Story called me to say she wanted to buy my column. The pay was only fifty dollars; was that okay? If she only knew that I would have paid *her* fifty bucks to get that first byline!

I snapped the paper shut and followed Rob into the new, trendy restaurant that he had been so eager to try. We had been dating for several months and I was crazy about him, but that evening, it was an effort to even pretend that I was still interested in having dinner at this pretentious eatery when all I could think of was that letter.

"This was satire. Light humor! How could she have missed that?" I asked Rob once we were seated.

"Maybe she's been sugar-deprived for too long?" he guessed, as we studied the menu.

"Why did they have to publish her stupid letter?" I groused. "Why didn't they publish a positive letter? Unless... what if this was the *only* letter they got?" As I considered this mortifying possibility, I surveyed my dinner options at this obscenely overpriced restaurant. *Lentil Tempeh Piccata.* Eww. *Stinging Nettle Aglonotti.* What in God's name was that? And *sugar* was supposed to be the big danger? I finally decided on *Wood-Fired Aubergine "Meat" Lasagna*, only after confirming that "aubergine" was eggplant. Rob ordered something involving kelp noodles with "feta." Maybe it's just me, but as a general rule I prefer eating foods that don't require scare quotes.

Rob agreed that the letter was ridiculous, but I had trouble getting over myself and must have been lousy company. My disappointment would fade, and the sale was still a breakthrough moment. Besides, newspapers like controversy and this letter gave it to them by punching through a parody with a grim reprimand. Additionally, I now had a good connection with the features editor—a valuable step up.

I was still hungry after our date. That mingy portion of "meat" lasagna barely made a dent in my overactive appetite. Back in my apartment I flung open the freezer and served myself a comforting bowl of chocolate mint ice cream, visualizing those feel-good endorphins cavorting through my brain receptors and flooding them with snappy new ideas for satire. I also pictured that letter writer curling up with a bowl of jicama sticks and low-fat Greek yogurt. It would serve her right.

The published essay had reflected many weeks of dedicated effort: writing, revising, consulting, and revising again. I wanted to master the art of the personal essay and had enrolled in an extension class at UCLA, taught by a successful writer whose work I followed closely through his columns in *Writer's Digest* magazine.

Good personal essays require different writing and storytelling skills than those required for hard news and features. Too often, writers are told by "experts" and often, publishers, that strong, salable personal essays require that they must show how they have changed somehow from an experience. Demonstrating change can be an excellent launching point but it's absurd to squeeze the personal essay into such a constricting box. It's about the execution of the writing more than the subject itself. Outstanding personal essays can reflect on an experience or even a small moment: an unexpected and meaningful exchange with a store clerk, the discovery of a new musical artist and how that music speaks to you, or a funny experience with kids that sheds light on a larger universal truth.

Personal essays also work when writers reveal enough of themselves to earn the reader's trust as a credible reporter. Their perspective must be thoughtful and evocative, and their voices must be authentic. Readers can usually sense a faker. All these elements will earn a reader's feeling of kinship and gratitude for the pleasure of having read the work of such writers. An outstanding personal essay might be remembered for years, perhaps even clipped and saved in a notebook.

In a persuasive essay, on the other hand, a reader needs to see compelling evidence supporting the writer's argument, and the writer must not badger, lecture, pander, or talk down to the reader. A credible persuasive essay will also acknowledge—fairly—arguments from the other side.

My instructor at UCLA offered solid feedback on this essay, but it was Marge, one of my favorite people at Creative Age, whose coaching added the grace notes that I knew had clinched the sale. In her early sixties, Marge was a great editor with a ready smile and upbeat personality. Those traits were doubtless essential in her line of work, because all day long she wrote about and edited articles about the extremely solemn topic of dialysis and transplantation.

Humor really needs to pop, but my initial drafts lacked the inventive prose that would bring it home. Marge kindly sat with me and discussed her suggestions. She had circled my flaccid, unimaginative words and phrases, recommending vibrant and surprising ones in their place. My ho-hum phrase "lying in the sauna" smartened up into "peacefully braising;" "rail-thin, muscled young woman" got a makeover to "willowy, taut and polished young woman." I loved Marge's ideas and understood what I had to do to up my game. She suggested I start reading S. J. Perelman, whom I had never heard of, but Perelman became an essential element of my humor writing education.

Here is the opening of Perelman's short story, "The Love Decoy: A Story of Youth in College Today—Awake, Fearless, Unashamed."

> "Professor Gompers is ill!" The whisper spread like wildfire through the packed classroom. A feeling of emulsion swept over me. Kindly old Professor Gompers, whose grizzled chin and chiseled grin had made his name a byword at Tuna Fish College for Women! Ivy Nudnick, sauciest co-ed in the class, she of the unruly locks and the candied gray eye, leaned over to impart the latest gossip.

I was gobsmacked by Perelman and his wicked inventiveness. His career spanned most of the twentieth century, during which he wrote short stories for *The New Yorker* along with books, plays and screenplays. Perelman's adapted screenplay for the film *Around the World in Eighty Days* earned an Academy Award in 1956. Never in a million years could I touch his skill level. He was also from my grandparents' generation, better educated than I was in history and literature. His genius at spinning ingeniously hilarious phrases and words—sometimes from French or Latin—greatly magnified my understanding of what was possible.

Perelman's career spanned the 1920s through the early 1970s, but I was reassured that his topics included such evergreens as customer complaints, health trends, romances gone wrong, and travel mishaps. Here's part of a line from the story, "What Am I

Doing Away from Home?" about the impossibility of getting a good night's sleep in a busy hotel: ". . . every so often somebody in the room overhead broke into a waltz clog in a pair of specially built lead shoes." Can't you just visualize the poor guy or gal in that room, coping with those clomping lead shoes?

Perelman was the first writer to inspire me to reach beyond my regular reading fare as a pathway to developing my own voice and perspective. His ingenious and visionary use of language taught me to always reach beyond what was comfortable in my own writing. I began keeping lists of more stimulating, surprising, lively words that felt real to my own sense of language. And as his own stories proved, technology may change but the human condition does not. I didn't have to produce groundbreaking topics—there's nothing new under the sun, as King Solomon observed more than two thousand years ago. What I could do was bring a voice and angle to them that was mine and mine alone.

Interviewing "The Big Man"

*The story I have told throughout my work life
I could not have told as well without Clarence.*
—Bruce Springsteen

In the face of romantic heartbreak, women have been known to cope in a variety of ways. Frequent crying is de rigueur, but you can only cry for so many hours a day before becoming dehydrated. Complementary activities may include overeating, undereating, shopping, gambling, or writing a memoir or novel, such as Cheryl Strayed's Wild (which requires really good hiking shoes). The less hearty among the sorrowful might slip away for a weekend cruise or spa visit.

Some women choose violence. After her second marriage imploded, my Aunt Eleanor wrenched the huge stuffed marlin that her ex had caught on a fishing expedition from above the fireplace, threw it down in the garage, and repeatedly ran over it with her Mercedes-Benz. This was not completely cathartic, but it was a start.

My teddy bear Harold was not quite enough comfort to heal my broken heart from my fizzled romance with Rob, despite Harold's quiet, constant affection. Even shedding copious tears on my therapist's couch didn't quite cure me of the blues. I needed something else. But what?

One day, I hit upon the insane idea that the best medicine for my achy-breaky heart would be to bag an interview with Clarence Clemons, the sax player with Bruce Springsteen's E Street Band. What did Clemons have to do with any of this? Just this: my ex, Rob, had been the first to introduce me to Springsteen's music, and from the first chords of *"Jungleland," "Rosalita," and of course, "Born in the USA,"* I was an instant addict. The themes of many Springsteen songs were far from my reality. I didn't grow up in an economically struggling town, didn't know anyone who worked on the highway, blasting through the bedrock, didn't hang out in bars, and had no ambition to drag race. Many songs were laced with an undercurrent of anger or anxiety; others were about dreams delayed or even deflated. Yet the songs were aspirational, shot through with passionate, irresistible youthful energy and a no-holds-barred determination to fulfill one's dreams wherever they took you once you escaped the "darkness at the edge of town."

I also had aspirations for my dream career and was also on fire to achieve them. And I longed to find the comfort of lasting love. Who among us didn't have a "hungry heart" when we were young? In this way, Springsteen's music moved me emotionally, and injected me with the joy of rock and roll abandon.

Clarence Clemons was a huge part of the magic of the E Street Band literally and figuratively. "The Big Man" was six foot two, wavering between two hundred fifty and three hundred pounds, and darker than a moonless night. Clarence played that saxophone with such passion—emotional highs and lows, playfulness, and lovable showmanship—that no one who ever watched the E Street Band play could ever forget the experience.

During our relationship, Rob had taken me to see Clarence perform in a Hollywood club with his own band, the Red Bank Rockers. The club setting allowed us to see the colossal musician up close in a band of his own creation. The lead singer, J. T. Bowen, belted out gospel-themed, bluesy rock songs in a gravelly timbre that reminded me of Otis Redding. We danced to the soulful rock, doing so as Clarence urged us to "surrender to the rock 'n roll DJ!" No job could have been easier. The music had flowed through me all during that fabulous evening.

Many months later, when I discovered that Clarence was scheduled for a promotional tour in Los Angeles to promote the Red Bank Rockers' first album, *Rescue*, I convinced myself that if I got this interview, it would reboot my emotional recovery, or "Jump Start My Heart," as he sang on his album. What a coup this would be!

However, there were a few trifling problems with this plan. First, it took outrageous chutzpah. My qualifications to write about one of the most famous sax players in the country were zero. I didn't know the difference between a tenor versus an alto sax, or which one Clarence played. I had no connections with anyone in the music industry. I could think of no magazine that would both be interested in Clarence Clemons yet also trust someone like me to write it. This was in 1983, when Springsteen and his E Street Band were an international phenomenon.

And even if my madcap scheme succeeded, my romance would not rise from the graveyard. True, I was a woman scorned, but I was filled with determination to show the ex that *I was going places*. I seemed to be going alone at this point, but I'd worry about that later.

I searched *Writer's Digest Marketplace*, a doorstop of a book that listed thousands of book and magazine publishers by category and region. Where to even begin? My only specialty was writing about elderly volunteers running the nation's hospital gift shops. Scrolling through the listings, I hoped to find a magazine needle in a haystack, one that would be eager for a story about Clarence but wouldn't be too picky about who was doing the writing. Having exhausted middle-brow publications, I began fishing at the lower rungs of the editorial barrel, the mags few had ever heard of and that paid a few pennies a word.

I decided to go about it from the other direction. If I could secure the interview first, the assignment would naturally follow. I called CBS Records and asked for the publicist handling the artist's press tour. After being connected with Angie, I said, "I'm a local writer and would like to schedule an interview with Mr. Clemons."

"And who are you writing for?"

"I've got some feelers out there, but I don't have the assignment fully firmed up. *Yet,*" I added with emphasis.

I heard a sigh on the other end of the receiver. "Call back if you get one," she said before hanging up.

Close to giving up, I found a listing for a Black men's magazine called *Players*. They did not mean gin rummy. By this point, I had no other conceivable options, but could I really debase myself by writing for a magazine like this—even assuming I could get the assignment?

You bet I could. It was my last hope.

I called the office, which happened to be right on Beverly Boulevard in the city, not far from my apartment. *Players* had a sizable readership and had published many Black writers of note, including Alex Haley and Julian Bond. Still, there was no skirting the issue that women wearing skirts were few and far between in the magazine's pages. I hoped that up in Heaven, Papa Cohen was too busy studying the Talmud to notice that his granddaughter, former editor of the Jewish student newspaper at UC Berkeley, was scoring a writing assignment for a naughty publication. My heart pounding, I asked to speak to the publisher, who took my call immediately. "This is Emory," he said in a Southern drawl.

I introduced myself and told him I could get an interview with Clarence Clemons if he wanted the story. "Would you like the story, Emory?"

"Yes, I want the story." He sounded very interested. "But what have you written? Show me some of your work." The next day, I brought him my humor essay from the *Herald-Examiner* and a few features from the magazine, including one on teamwork and another called "What Does Your Uniform Say About You?" That might not have been the best choice. There weren't many uniforms on the models in *Players* magazine. Yet Emory reviewed my clips and called to give me the go-ahead. Mazel tov! I had just landed my first X-rated journalism assignment.

I called CBS and tried to hide my smirk when Angie came on the line. "I've got the assignment," I told her, faking nonchalance, as if I interviewed rock stars all the time.

"Yeah? Who for?" I told her the name of the magazine, prepared to hear her say, "Never heard of it" before hanging up on me again. Instead, she repeated the name in a matter-of-fact tone of voice as she jotted it down, then told me the date and time to arrive at the studios for the interview. Barbara, my editor, had been witness to all these personal calls I had been making on company time.

"I did it!" I shouted in a loud whisper, as our office door was open.

"You go, girl!" she said, both of us grinning.

I sat there in a daze, not quite believing my pie-in-the-sky scheme was actually working. A week later, CBS called, and my heart sank. They must have discovered my deception of passing myself off as a music writer and had called to cancel my interview. Instead, my interview location had moved from the studios to Mr. Clemons' hotel room in West Hollywood. This felt vaguely unsettling.

A few days later, I was watching an interview with Clarence on television with my mom and sister. I had been excited for my mom to see "The biggest man you've ever seen!" as Springsteen sometimes introduced him on stage, but I hadn't really thought this through too carefully. As soon as his huge, intimidating-looking presence filled the screen, complete with Panama hat and a suspicious-looking earring, I looked at my mother and watched the color drain from her face.

"You are NOT going to his hotel room!" she thundered. Mom rarely thundered, so this was serious.

"Oh, come on, Mom!" I tried to humor her. "Journalists do interviews with celebrities in hotel rooms all the time!" (Did they? I had no idea. It didn't seem like a good idea to me, either, less and less so the longer I had to think about it.)

I hated to make my mom worry, but this was my excellent journalism adventure, and nobody was going to deprive me of it. Walking down the carpeted hallway to Clarence's room I was so jittery

I was afraid my voice would bobble when I spoke to him. Did I have the right questions planned? Would my tape recorder work? Would he possibly try to get frisky if there was enough time between interviews?

I floated down the carpeted hallway, still in a state of disbelief that I was about to interview one of the most famous saxophone players in the country. I knocked on his hotel room door as my heart knocked very loudly in my chest. He greeted me with a sweet smile and was patient when I asked him if he would mind stopping the interview after only one minute while I double- and triple-checked that my recorder was working (it was an ongoing paranoia of mine). He told the famous story about the night he'd first met Bruce Springsteen in a little club in Asbury Park. It was a windy night, and as Clemons opened the door holding his saxophone, he took the door clean off the place. When he asked Springsteen if he could play for him, the answer was a swift yes. No arguing with a man who can pull a door off its hinges when he strides into the room!

He also spoke at length about the racism he had endured throughout his career, including in the early days of performing with Springsteen, and how many producers had told him that his music for his solo album sounded "too Black." The rock industry "was like a bleached blonde. They don't want their Black roots to show . . . you don't hear the rhythm and blues," he said.

Clarence Clemons made it easy for me to do my job, which was a feel-good story for a Black men's magazine about a phenomenally talented Black musician man who had succeeded despite the odds. The editor wasn't hungry for sophisticated questions about the music industry, questions I wasn't knowledgeable enough to ask anyway. When I rose to thank Clemons and leave, he leaned in just close enough to give me what I'd call "an air hug."

When the magazine was out on the street, I couldn't wait to see it yet also dreaded having to find it. At a local newsstand, I asked, shamefaced, if they had *Players* magazine. He pointed to the section of the newsstand where naughty magazines lived in infamy behind a curtain. Well, the magazine wasn't going to levitate and fly into my hands, so I tentatively tugged the curtain aside an inch and peeked. The coast was clear. I slipped behind that curtain and quickly spotted the only magazine featuring a Black woman on the cover. I paid for the magazine, which the newsagent sensitively slipped into a brown paper wrapper.

In my apartment, I opened the magazine to discover they had given my story a three-page spread, with a full-page photo of The Big Man. It was real! I was thrilled and mortified in equal measure. I had to cover up an unmentionable cartoon on the third page before making copies of the article and sending it to all my friends—and to Rob. After all, nobody I knew had a subscription.

I tried to imagine the look on Rob's face when he saw the story. I guessed that he'd think I was slightly nuts and that he was well rid of me. I didn't care. I enjoyed a delicious sense of satisfaction that through this wild writing escapade, I had regained a sense of self. And when I showed the article to my teddy bear Harold, he was, as always, the picture of admiration.

Chasing Bylines from Westwood to Washington, DC

In its dreams, good journalism longs for an honest mind at either end of the transaction.
—Lance Morrow, *The Age of Typewriters*

After a year and a half at Creative Age Publishing, I craved deeper, more demanding work in healthcare writing. I got that opportunity at UCLA, where I was hired to write a variety of articles, profiles, news, and feature releases for the entire health sciences complex. This was a big step up for me. No more punching an ancient time clock, listening to the boss howling about the electricity bill, or gasping for oxygen in the typesetting room where Brian, our gentle giant of a typesetter, miraculously set all but perfect type while squinting through the thick haze of smoke that coiled all day long from the ever-present cigarette half-dangling from his lips. I continued to think of Carol with gratitude for having provided an ideal launching point for my journalism career.

Walking to my interviews throughout the hospital or the health sciences complex, I proudly wore my badge identifying me as a WRITER (in all capital letters) at UCLA Hospital and Clinics. I was employed by the Health Sciences Communications Department, which produced the grad school alumni magazines as well as articles and press materials for med center publications or trade magazines.

This was unambiguously public relations work, often considered as second- or even third-rate compared to straightforward journalism. This didn't bother me because I had always had a fascination with medicine. My complete lack of aptitude in science and math ensured I would never become a doctor, but I could at least *write* about the fascinating world of medicine. Cece's radical career had stimulated my early interest in alternative healthcare, but I wasn't a purist. I had always believed in fusing the best of allopathic and alternative healing methods. If my mandate was to make UCLA doctors, nurses, social workers, psychologists, researchers, graduate students, administrators, deans, programs, and donors look good, I was on it.

It happened to be an especially exciting time when I joined the department. I interviewed the foremost researcher who had linked the BRCA gene to the development of breast cancer. I wrote about a large-scale study on the causes and patterns of homelessness, already a growing problem nationally, and my cover story on the subject for the School of Public Health's alumni magazine was picked up internationally. I wrote about the link between creativity and bipolar disorder and helped promote a concert featuring works of such brilliant bipolar composers, including Handel, Schumann, Berlioz, and Mahler. These stories were all media hits, capturing dozens of pickups, which is what we lived for. When UCLA started its air ambulance program, I hitched a ride in the helicopter, excited and just a wee bit nervous as we lifted off from the helipad on the hospital roof for a quick spin around the neighborhood.

My first day on the job, I was bouncing with energy and eager to please. My editor, Judi, asked if I felt ready to go and interview a professor in the School of Dentistry who managed the maxillofacial clinic and surgeries. I had never even heard the word "maxillofacial," so Judi explained that this work involved reconstructive surgery of the face, the oral cavity, head, neck, and jaw. Maxillofacial patients might have had cancers of the head or neck, congenital abnormalities, or been in accidents.

"I should warn you, it could be a little intense," she said. "I can give you a different assignment if you want."

"I'm ready!" I exclaimed. And so, girded with my notebook, pen, tape recorder, and raw inexperience, off I marched down the warren of subterranean hallways of the medical center and out toward the adjacent School of Dentistry. The professor of maxillofacial surgery ushered me into his office and dimmed the lights as he began a slide show of *before* and *after* photos of patients who had gone under the knife.

The gruesome *before* slides made me go all queasy and weak. People were missing significant portions of their faces, or they had been catastrophically rearranged. As the surgeon explained the slides, I scribbled notes as fast as I could, gripping my pen so hard that my script shriveled to a tiny, cramped, illegible tangle of ink. The surgeon cheerfully explained each case, becoming more animated with each *after* photo. "Now, look at this guy here," he urged me to consider one slide. "Never saw that truck coming. Lucky to be alive."

Lucky to be alive, I scrawled. "But look at the jaw reconstruction after only three surgeries," he boasted in a jaunty tone. I nodded, grateful my stomach was empty. I realized that healthcare professionals had to maintain some emotional distance to do their jobs, and I wondered what it took to absorb the sights of these devastatingly damaged faces as simply all in a day's work. When the slide show was mercifully over, I thanked the doctor for his time. Walking back to my office, I was sure I had blown this first assignment, having been too shocked to have grasped the most important things he had explained to me.

When Judi saw my ashen expression, she apologized profusely for having thrown me into the deep end on my first day. But as usual, I had claimed a readiness and competence beyond my abilities. Somehow, I survived my trial by fire, and with some help from Judi, my article was approved and published to the surgeon's satisfaction. A few months later, I had no problem facing down an assignment about forensic dentistry and how grisly crime and accident victims were sometimes so unrecognizable that positive identifications could be made only by their teeth. Yeah, I could do that now.

Judi was a great editor and mentor, and a lot of fun to be around. I admired her excellent organizational and editing skills, but perhaps the most valuable lesson she modeled was how to keep her sense of humor when demanding "customers"—the professors or deans with outsized egos whose schools we were promoting—called with their insatiable demands for more media coverage. Judi was always gracious and tactful while managing their expectations, and after she got off one of those calls, she'd roll her eyes and laugh as she told me about the latest "request" to add to an individual's glory and renown.

My new boss, John, was also great, clear about his expectations, which were always reasonable, and also available for advice when I needed it. A highlight of my week was meeting with John every Monday morning for a brief tête-à-tête at my desk. John kept these appointments with everyone in the department, which I thought was brilliant. After asking me if I had any concerns about any of my assignments, the agenda was wide open. We'd end up talking about anything and everything, from the best gyros he ever ate in his native town of Chicago to new music favorites to how we rated the latest coffee flavor we brewed each morning in the office. Few things were as vital to the smooth running of our department as an outstanding cup of joe for everyone at eight-thirty in the morning. Our standing Monday morning huddles not only kept lines of communication open, but also made me feel integral to our department work.

Our office environment was so much more professional than that of the slightly kooky publishing company. Everyone was congenial, team-oriented, professional and friendly. I suspected that this could be the best job I ever would get and that I should try to keep it forever. Besides, as a state-funded operation, the pay and benefits were also primo. And yet, despite having landed in professional clover, I wanted to earn a master's degree in journalism like Judi had. Only a few years older than me, Judi encouraged me to go for it because it would provide me with incomparable training to report and write rapidly, which would always serve me well. With mixed feelings about leaving a job I loved and wondering if I even really needed this piece of sheepskin, I applied to the best programs in the country: Columbia and Northwestern.

I hoped I'd be a shoo-in for Columbia, though the editing and writing admissions tests they administered were tougher than I expected. Still optimistic, I sang "New York, New York," in my apartment, hamming it up with my arms thrown wide during the chorus, imagining myself back in Manhattan as a much savvier grad student than the naïf who'd fallen for three-card monte on Lexington Avenue just a few years before.

As winter turned to spring, I anxiously checked my mail each day, looking for that big fat acceptance envelope from Columbia. Instead, a thin envelope contained the news that I had been waitlisted—an admissions limbo where you could still slide into a seat in the class if a fully accepted candidate backed out. Unwilling to wait to see if I would get lucky, I gratefully accepted Northwestern's clear invitation to join the class. I retired "New York, New York" from my playlist and began singing "Chicago (That Toddlin' Town)." Northwestern's Medill School of Journalism was a top-rated program, and I was eager to explore the great city of Chicago for the first time, including its fabulous music scene, famous stuffed pizza, Sears Tower, the consumer glories of Michigan Avenue, and the beautiful Evanston campus.

Boarding the plane, though, I was filled with tearful buyer's remorse. Why was I leaving a wonderful job, friends, a great apartment, and perhaps most significantly, my boyfriend, Jeff? I had met him shortly after he had moved to LA from Chicago, and we had hit it off right away. He was trying to get himself established in a business career, while I already had a couple of years of full-time writing under my belt and had begun applying to grad school. But now that I was in the best romance of my life, my paperwork at school was signed, sealed, and delivered. I had taken out student loans. I was buckling my seat belt for a yearlong mystery ride.

Dragging my suitcase into my shoebox of a dorm room, I felt like I had been demoted from business class to steerage. The walls, dark and dreary, were riveted with a thousand pinpricks where prior tenants had tacked up posters and pictures. My window faced the parking lot and the "El" train tracks and platform. This was a depressing comedown from my spacious, light-filled apartment in Los Angeles, where my living room sliding-glass doors let the sunshine in each day on our tree-lined street.

For therapy, I walked throughout Evanston, enchanted by the old, beautiful, stately homes along Sheridan Road that hugged the campus. These walks were a feast for the eyes and restored my tranquility. The streets in the college town had a quaint yet upscale feel, and I found plenty to keep me entertained outside of school and my part-time job in the school's library. I went out to lunch occasionally with a classmate at a cozy diner, splurged on impossibly rich, creamy gelato at another café, and tucked myself for hours inside Bookman's Alley, a fabulously cramped and slightly musty used bookstore where I made dozens of literary discoveries and frequent purchases. The store specialized in antiquarian books, and the day I spotted a century-old boxed set of the complete works of Shakespeare in miniature for only seventy-five bucks, I thought it was a steal and wrote a check. The pages of the three-inch high volumes were gilt-edged, bound in velvety soft green leather softened through sixty years of touch, and the print was still crisp. Holding the smooth, Lilliputian volumes in my hands, I felt a sense of both history and publishing artistry.

Most of my instructors were tough journalists of the old school—current or former reporters, art and theater critics, and editors at the nation's top newspapers and magazines. We were all shocked that on our first day in reporting class, the classroom was still equipped with old-fashioned typewriters! Computers had long graced the school's modern downtown newsroom but inexplicably had not arrived in Evanston. Professor Paul McGrath made no apologies. A former investigative reporter for both the *Chicago Sun-Times* and the *Chicago Tribune*, he had come of age as a journalist when Steve Jobs had been playing in the sandbox. Defending the use of typewriters, he said, "If the power goes out while you're working on a computer, you're finished. A typewriter will never fail you."

My professional experience gave me an advantage in grad school, but the pressure of daily reporting lit a fire under my feet. With few exceptions, we had to identify a story to cover, track down sources and facts, and write the piece in the same day. During the winter I covered legal issues, fishing for my "catch of the day" by sifting through the latest legal filings in Chicago's main courthouse. With my target chosen—another lawsuit over a slip-and-fall on the city's frozen streets or an intriguing case involving a suspected insurance scam—I headed to the downtown newsroom, picked up the phone and started calling potential sources for my story. It was rare for anyone to turn me down even though I was a student. Medill had an outstanding reputation and ran its own news service, so our reporting was published regularly in subscribed regional papers across the country.

This was also my first real winter, a shivering shock to a lifelong Californian. One morning I stood on the train platform waiting for the El to whisk me downtown for my day's reporting. Wearing open-toed slides and a lightweight California jacket totally absurd for Chicago in January, I hugged myself to try to keep from freezing over. A classmate waited next to me, the son of an auto executive from Dearborn, Michigan, who was sensibly if luxuriously dressed in an elegant wool coat, wool scarf, and polished leather shoes. With the wind blowing and the temperature in the midthirties, he looked warm and rich. Throughout the snowy day, I trembled with cold, slipping and sliding through the city in my absurdly unsuitable frostbite-inviting shoes. After I had turned in my story, I practically skated over to Marshall Field to invest in a real winter coat and my first pair of winter boots.

Other than wearing open-toed shoes in the snow, my attire and behavior were unremarkable, almost boring. This confused several Midwesterners who expected a native Californian to be a bit flamboyant, outrageous, maybe have purple and green hair or carry a mandolin or a surfboard around. I faced this disappointment so often that I sold a humor column about it to the *Chicago Tribune*, the first of several essays I sold to the paper that year.

Journalism school wasn't only about reporting. We had classes covering legal issues such as libel, intellectual property, and plagiarism. (The plagiarism class came too late for one student, who at the beginning of the year turned in a story cribbed from a Chicago newspaper. He was summarily thrown out of the program.) There are always gray areas in the law defining the boundaries for libel and intellectual property, and this was a fascinating area of discussion in class from a moral and ethical standpoint.

One day, we were discussing "the public's right to know" and how journalists and editors define it. This discussion quickly became an unexpectedly painful and memorable experience. Our instructor held up a page from one of the Chicago dailies for us all to see. The page featured a large photo of the victim at the scene of a fatal car accident, his body covered by a sheet on a gurney. Was the newspaper within its rights to publish this tragic photo, or had it pushed the boundaries too far? Having opened the class with these questions, students tumbled over one another to weigh in with their opinions.

Most of my classmates argued emphatically that the paper was correct to publish the photo under that nebulous value of "the public's right to know." I was among the minority who disagreed, citing a needless intrusion on the family's privacy, an exploitation of private grief. Listening to the naïve, callous, and cavalier arguments by those applauding the publishing decision, I felt almost sick with reignited grief. I wondered if any of them could have maintained their positions had they ever faced such a tragedy in their own families.

I had. This issue was personal for me. My brother, Allan, had died in a car accident at the age of seventeen when his car careened off Mulholland Drive in Los Angeles. The fabled, scenic road follows the ridgeline of the eastern Santa Monica Mountains, and in its most dangerous loop it twists and turns like a snake. David Lynch's thriller *Mulholland Drive* begins with a scene of a fiery head-on collision on this road.

I was nine years old when our family suffered this shocking and overwhelming tragedy. The newspaper account about Allan's death had published his recent high school graduation photo, where my brother looked so handsome and dignified. I couldn't even begin to imagine the added anguish for my family if the newspaper had instead chosen sensationalism and published a photo of his body covered by a sheet on a gurney.

Students who argued in favor of the accident scene photo cited a possible public good: it could make people who were reckless drivers be more careful. But would that potential benefit counterbalance the certain harm of pouring a river of salt into a family of broken hearts? Might it needlessly hype the fears among the already fearful? Realizing that my view was a minority opinion, I felt emotionally drained and depressed after class. In a few short years many of these classmates would become editors making publishing decisions in newsrooms or television stations all over the country, greenlighting such coverage. As the saying goes in journalism, "If it bleeds, it leads."

Journalism is a craft. For the especially talented and industrious it can become an art. But it is not a science and never can be. The media create and shape messages through the stories they choose to cover and which they choose to ignore. They also angle their stories by selecting whom to interview, therefore providing a platform for cherry-picked views, and whom they avoid questioning, not wanting to share their perspectives. Stories are shaped and molded in myriad ways, including the images they publish, the pull quotes in large type, the headlines with biases baked in. Most people drawn to journalism are idealistic, pulled toward this career because we want our writing to have impact. Political and social biases in journalism were as old as journalism itself, but these biases were increasingly and unapologetically on display and driving the media agenda. More and more, this agenda took precedence against the ideal of aiming for objectivity, impossible as this was to achieve.

I brought my own biases to my work as well. For example, for one assignment we were to debate a topical issue with another student, arguing our cases in front of the entire class. Based on my experience at UCLA, I argued in favor of animal research in medicine, facing off against a classmate arguing against it. As I expected, her arguments were thin and sentimental, well-intentioned but naïve and even wrong. I agreed that animal research needed guardrails against abuse of animals and to avoid needless duplication of efforts. Ultimately, I argued, the question was really basic: whose lives did we value more, those of the sheep, pigs, and mice, or our own human lives?

"Look around the room," I asked during the debate. "Without decades of careful medical research involving animals that delivered consistent results, some of us might not have survived childhood influenza or other illnesses. Others among us might have polio or been debilitated by viral illnesses that we were protected from through vaccines." My debate partner became very quiet.

I spent my last quarter of the program in Washington, DC, where affordable housing for a student like me was scarce. It had taken weeks to find a rental in my budget, a bedroom in a private home. Over the phone with the landlady I had agreed to pay for two full months upon arrival. But when I arrived with my suitcase at the modest, two-story house on the edge of the Washington-Maryland border, I encountered a middle-aged woman whose demeanor was a tad deranged. Consistent with this appearance, the living room was funereally dark, the curtains drawn. The furniture had the snowy appearance of not having been dusted in years. Over the phone, the landlady had sounded sane, but she and her house gave me the creeps. Spooked, I told her I had changed my mind and only wanted to stay one week.

She became agitated. "Oh no," she said. "You pay now for the two months you agreed to, or you don't stay for a single night," she said.

No rational person would have handed over the money. Danger floated in the dust-mote-mottled air. But I didn't want to call my parents and ask for help. They lived on a tight budget as it was, though they surely would have been appalled at the prospect of their younger daughter bunking down with Rochester's wife and unquestionably would have helped me had I asked. But I didn't want to be a burden or worry them—I'd worry enough for all three of us. I couldn't afford a hotel even for a few nights and had already failed to find any affordable other rentals near a Metro. With nowhere else to go and quivering with nervousness, I handed over my hard-earned money, Jackson after Jackson, until her fists were full.

I bumped my suitcase up the faded steps to my tiny room. The small chest of drawers was dusty too. When was the last time this lunatic had any tenants at all? The adjacent bedrooms were empty; I seemed to be alone in the haunted house. Hoping to never see my landlady (who lived in her basement), I tiptoed downstairs each morning and tiptoed up the stairs each night. Even when another woman rented the room next to mine, I always felt a little scared living there. Though I had kitchen privileges, I chose to buy sandwiches at a small, cheerful café in the shopping mall two blocks away instead. Living with a nutcase just might have been the first real dangerous reporting zone I'd experienced, but it was a price I was willing to pay as I earned my professional chops.

In our newsroom in downtown Washington, I was stunned to learn that the Medill News Service didn't already have an established beat in healthcare. I asked for and received permission to create one, covering stories about government programs to expand mental health services in rural areas, FDA regulations, child-safety campaigns, and dozens of other health-related topics. I loved watching my published clips arrive steadily from the *Great Falls Tribune*, the *North Jersey Herald News*, *The Oak Ridger*, the *Biloxi Sun-Herald,* and my most reliable fan, the *Idaho State Journal,* serving Pocatello-Chubbuck counties.

At a press briefing I attended about the latest findings on the AIDS virus, Surgeon General Dr. C. Everett Koop took questions from the audience after making his initial statement. In my excitement to be with the big-league reporters, I shot my hand up in the auditorium filled with about five hundred people. I did not expect to be noticed. I was only a Medill student! When the surgeon general pointed to me, I was so stunned that I froze, utterly and devastatingly. What was my question? It had vaporized. As hundreds of people stared at me, I sat mute and humiliated. Dr. Koop glared at me from under his thatch of salt-and-pepper eyebrows for two seconds, then pointed to a real reporter who knew what they wanted to say.

Hanging my head in shame as I waited for the Metro, I spotted Marlene Cimons, a longtime medical writer from the *Los Angeles Times,* waiting for the same train. I recognized her because she still wore her name tag from the press event, and I perked up. I read Cimons's work avidly and stared at her out of the corner of my eye like a groupie casting a mesmerized gaze at a rock star idol. I decided to introduce myself and tell her how much I admired her work, then confessed how stupid I felt over my moment of self-immolation. She didn't exactly ooze sympathy but was coolly journalistic, shrugging and saying it was no big deal, hardly a career killer. She spoke to me with no hint of condescension or pity, and by the time I exited the train I decided that I hadn't just destroyed my nascent career. Boy, I still had a lot to learn in this field, not least of which was more humility.

Planning a Career, Planning a Life

I am a Jew because, knowing the story of my people, I hear their call to write the next chapter ... only if I remain a Jew will the story of a hundred generations live on in me. I continue their journey because, having come this far, I may not let it and them fail. I cannot be the missing letter in the scroll.
—Rabbi Jonathan Sacks,
former chief rabbi of the United Congregation of the Commonwealth, *A Letter in the Scroll.*

Throughout my year in grad school, I spent almost as much time thinking about my personal future as my professional one. When I had left for Chicago, my relationship with Jeff had been at a crossroads. Raised as a secular Jew, Jeff had become enthralled by Orthodox Judaism after college, and during our courtship he was exploring our shared faith through attending Torah classes with an Orthodox rabbi. Growing up, Jeff's religion had been sports. He had been the fastest kid on the high school track team and played baseball. His family made annual, perfunctory visits to their synagogue for the High Holidays, and like kids from many other Reform Jewish families, Jeff's formal Jewish education had ended when the last tables were cleared after his bar mitzvah party.

Jeff's father, Robert, had arrived in the United States in 1938 as a six-year-old refugee from Germany. Like many first-generation immigrants, he was satisfied with achieving freedom from persecution as well as the opportunity to work and provide for his family in the United States. Indeed, Robert (born Lothar) Gruen became a successful textile salesman and supported his family in a comfortable middle-class life in Northbrook, Illinois. Intuitively, Jeff understood that there was something more to life than the privileges of Western, material comfort. But he didn't know what questions to ask or whom to ask. That changed through an unexpected and improbable friendship with a religious Christian named Charlie during Jeff's junior year abroad program in Lancaster, England.

Charlie couldn't believe that Jeff had no interest in going to Israel, the Holy Land, and pushed him to check it out during spring break. In Jerusalem, Jeff was invited to a traditional Shabbat dinner and to attend classes at Aish HaTorah, whose founder, Rabbi Noach Weinberg, lived with a burning mission to rescue unaffiliated Jews from what he considered a "spiritual holocaust" that was ending the Jewish line in thousands of families. By the time we met, Jeff was certain that the unspoken questions he'd carried for so long were right there in his own spiritual backyard. He was attending weekly classes on the Torah reading (*parsha*) of the week with Rabbi Daniel Lapin, an Orthodox rabbi originally from South Africa, reading books on classic Jewish philosophy and practice, and very slowly and guardedly, adopting a few religious practices.

Our conversations had flowed easily from the moment we met, and we shared many interests: Israel, British humor, building our careers, politics, books. Except for the occasional corny joke that caused inevitable eye-rolling, I liked his wry sense of humor—he made me laugh, which was a vital quality. From the start, he felt like a longtime friend, and I had never had that feeling of connection and comfort with any other man. It was a shame that he was flirting with Orthodoxy. I hoped he'd get over it soon.

Through the early months of our courtship, Jeff never suggested that I "should" begin to keep Shabbat to a greater degree. While practically speaking this would have been easy, as I did nothing, he was wise enough to know that any sort of "preaching" would make me defensive and alienate me. Still, once I acknowledged that I knew very, very little about what our faith taught, he encouraged me to attend classes with him. My own religious education had been more substantial than Jeff's, but until I started attending these classes, I hadn't realized the extent to which Judaism had been watered down and filtered through a twentieth-century, politically progressive lens.

The most shocking realization was learning that Judaism believes in an eternal soul that lives on after our physical lives have ended—that the souls of our loved ones will actually reside close to God in what Judaism calls the World of Truth. This knowledge would have been an enormous comfort to me and undoubtedly also to several relatives and family friends after my brother had died. While nothing really "comforts" so close to the moment of loss, eventually comfort would have arrived by being able to picture my beloved brother still living on in a realm I could not imagine, close to God. In the afterlife, or World of Truth, all accounts are balanced for our deeds performed in our physical lives.

Just whose idea was it to delete this essential concept from the Jewish syllabus? I quickly discovered that friends with similar backgrounds to mine, also now studying Torah concepts, similarly felt cheated of this fundamental Jewish belief. We find and fulfill our purpose and mission through our physical lives, knowing that there is eventual justice in the World of Truth is a huge comfort for the difficulties and suffering we endure. I had also basked in the fuzzy, warm emotion connected to the Jewish concept of *tikkun olam*, "fixing" or "repairing" the world. The phrase was long associated with universalist and social justice causes and feel-good activities, such as picking up trash on the beach or volunteering in a soup kitchen. Those are both excellent things—but they are not what the original concept meant.

Since the Enlightenment, opinions among Jews about how best

to repair the world had diverged. For the most part, Orthodoxy maintained that by following God's laws, our actions as individuals in being loyal to the mitzvoth "paid it forward" through universal blessings. But the Reform Movement shunned the particularism of the commandments and embraced universalism instead. As a result, as the late chief rabbi of the United Kingdom, Rabbi Jonathan Sacks wrote, "Every phrase associated with the idea of Tikkun Olam, phrases like 'light unto the nations,' or 'the Jewish mission,' or 'ethical universalism,' all those things became code words for assimilation, reform, and the whole concept of Tikkun Olam became suspect. What a tragedy that is today."

I began to understand that traditional Jewish notions of making the world a better place depended on following God's commandments. This would first improve my own behavior, and the goodness that flowed from that would flow outward, creating a ripple effect in my family, community, and society.

Modernization may have felt right and the logical path to sustaining Jewish identity in the melting pot of America, but three generations later, the Conservative and Reform movements in which we grew up were bleeding members. A majority of Jews from those movements were either melting away completely into secular society or choosing a new-found religious connection redolent of their grandparents' or great-grandparents' generations.

I saw very clearly the rapid slide of assimilation among our people. It concerned me in a generalized, vague way, but not forcefully enough that I felt any responsibility to actually do something about it. While I fretted that Orthodox Jewish principles would conflict with my feminist values and self-image, my feminism only went so far. I thirsted with ambition for a writing career, but I thirsted equally for marriage to a Jewish man who wanted to raise kids who would grow up and want to stay Jewish, too.

As the months rolled on, not only did Jeff fail to overcome his flirtation; he started to fall in love. Increasingly captivated by

Torah Judaism's profound teachings and the welcoming embrace of a community whose members—mostly young couples and singles—began inviting him for Shabbat and holiday meals, Jeff began to feel a sense of belonging. Despite my wariness over his growing involvement, how could I ignore our great chemistry, our shared values, and the fun we had together? He was a man of character, depth, and refinement—a very appealing bundle of traits, handsomely packaged. My heart had already been broken enough times by men who were all wrong for me.

I admired Jeff for his heartfelt desire to live a rich spiritual life, and while we could speak very easily on most topics, when the topic turned to religion things it often got prickly. "If God is real and the Torah is true," he'd ask, "aren't we obligated to follow it? If Jews like us continue to assimilate as our parents and grandparents did, who will be left to carry on our traditions?" I thought about this as I reached for another slice of cheese pizza at our favorite Italian restaurant. I needed time to chew on that in more ways than one. Was there kosher pizza here in LA, I wondered? And if so, would it—could it—taste this good?

Inconvenient as Jeff's theological questions were, I understood that they were crucial for me to grapple with. He was the first person to ask me directly what sort of Jewish life I visualized in my future. Would my commitment extend to real study and practice, as opposed to the fuzzy, intangible emotional connection I embraced? We were both young and defining our life paths, so it was the right time for these probing discussions. Sometimes I found them polarizing. Sometimes I found them paralyzing. But in the process of these conversations, increasingly uncomfortable for me, I learned something hugely significant and humbling: I was planning my career with meticulous care, envisioning where I wanted it to lead, step by step. But I was only planning a career. Jeff was planning a life.

After nine months of dating, during the summer before I left for Chicago I finally agreed to attend Torah classes with Jeff. These were line-by-line explications of the Five Books of Moses that by turns I found astonishing, dazzling, and troubling. Yet none of this stopped me from sparring with Jeff after class, sitting in a coffee shop over a slice of blueberry pie and cups of decaf as I aimed to puncture anything that Rabbi Lapin said that offended my UC Berkeley sensitivities.

Jeff parried with his new understanding of Torah philosophy, but he often shared my skepticism about certain laws or concepts that were very foreign to our modern sensibilities. He also promised to investigate those issues further to make sure he understood what was being taught. Torah scholars and even serious Torah-observant laypeople devoted a lifetime to plumbing the depths of meaning in the *Chumash,* the Five Books of Moses, as well as other sacred works.

Rabbi Lapin would quote the most famous ancient Jewish commentators, such as Rashi and Rambam, in the present tense. This startled me so much that I asked him to explain the reason behind it. "Rashi and many other sages are just as alive and relevant to us now as they were when they lived centuries ago, or even more than a thousand years ago," he said, his keen blue eyes meeting my challenging gaze. The idea that the ancients were considered so present tense prompted some of the first stirrings of humility regarding my lack of Jewish knowledge. Devoted to becoming a writer of excellence and to mastering my use of the English language to the best of my abilities, I was thrilled by Hebrew—its precision, psychological insights, and nuances.

For example, the word *shalom* is most widely understood to mean "peace" as well as a greeting for "hello." But by examining where else it appears in the Torah, shalom can also mean completeness, harmony, compensation, and even retribution. That last meaning may seem jarring, totally at odds with the other meanings, until one considers this truth: a person who has been violated in some way cannot be made whole or complete without seeing justice done.

Curiosity was essential to a journalist's work, and I believed I had it in bountiful measure when it came to researching my stories.

Could I dare to park that curiosity outside the front cover of a *Chumash* and refuse to look for the story behind the story of my own people? Of my own God?

I began to see that I needed more skin in the game beyond writing on Jewish topics from a journalistic remove. It wasn't enough to feel a love for Israel; wasn't enough to write my master's thesis on the early days of the Yiddish Press in America; wasn't enough to ride the Metro every Saturday morning during my summer in Washington, DC to attend an egalitarian Orthodox synagogue because I heard that the legendary writer Herman Wouk often prayed there, and I wanted to see him in person. That summer, I had read his novel, *Inside, Outside* and written him a fan letter via his New York publisher. He'd thrilled me by typing a gracious response on a small, elegantly embossed card. Though it was only a few lines acknowledging my fandom, I read it over and over again. Something must already have begun shifting inside me, because at the Orthodox egalitarian minyan I didn't feel as alien as I expected. I was, however, disappointed never to see the legendary writer in attendance.

It took many months for me to honestly face myself. The faith I felt so connected to emotionally had virtually no solid intellectual or theological underpinnings. Like so many of my friends, I felt I was "Jewish enough." I chose Jewish journalism in college. I turned down offers to date gentile men. I loved bagels (though inexplicably, not lox) and Chinese food!

Jeff's "big picture" questions about what would constitute a viable, rewarding, and sustainable Jewish life struck deep. As we braved our first tentative discussions about marriage, I had another realization. This wasn't only our immediate futures that were at stake. This was bigger than just me—or us—if, ultimately, there would be an us. On a macro, communal, and historical level, the future of my children, grandchildren, and great-grandchildren depended on how I would choose to answer these questions, the most significant and defining questions of my life.

During our year apart, we spoke several times a week and wrote lengthy letters to each other faithfully once a week. Jeff visited me twice in Chicago, taking me to his old neighborhood in Northbrook, showing me the house where he grew up and the huge, grassy expanse behind it where he played after school until his mother called him in for dinner. On a whim, we knocked on the door of one of his favorite neighbors, Mrs. DeAngelo, a warm and bubbly Italian who still lived on the block and who was genuinely delighted by the surprise visit. She showed us photos of her children, who, like Jeff, were all grown now. I showed Jeff around the Evanston campus and downtown we traversed State Street, dipping into jazz clubs and eating deep-dish Chicago pizza. We also ate an astonishing volume of gigantic pancakes at the famed pancake house, Walker Brothers, on the North Shore.

He told me more about the people he was getting to know in Venice, enjoying Shabbat meals with them as well as joining them on picnics or hikes together. Clearly, he felt increasingly connected to this small, thriving community. He was also increasingly clear that he wanted this Shomer Shabbat, kosher life, where regular Torah study was considered the mark of a growing Jew. The appeal became clearer and clearer to me as well, but often, on my solo walks along Sheridan Road, I wondered. Despite all the promise of spiritual, intellectual, and emotional gifts, would I feel too penned in by this life's restrictions? I couldn't imagine giving up eating at nonkosher restaurants—would I have to, and when? Would I be bored on Shabbat without my usual diversions of shopping, entertainment, writing, and calling friends?

Once again I faced a painful truth. Every other Jewish classmate in my program was secular. This was unsurprising yet now, with my growing awareness about Judaism's importance—on a personal and communal level—it also felt depressing. I was secular, too. The only difference between my classmates and myself was that (as far as I could tell) I was the only one wrestling with what a more fully engaged religious Jewish life would look like—and why it mattered.

Of my few friends at school, one was named Kathy, a religious Catholic who attended Mass twice a week. She told me about her effort to discuss the existence of God with another Jewish classmate with whom she was very friendly. When she told me of his childish and arrogant response ("If there's really a God, let him make some thunder right now!") I was embarrassed. Maybe I wasn't as arrogant as he was, but how different from him was I really? My sympathy for Jewish tradition and religious practice was severely limited. I recognized in myself some of the anti-Orthodox prejudice that I disliked in my classmates.

I loved Jeff. Could I also love keeping Shabbat, give up wearing jeans, and learn how to make a brisket that could become legendary in future generations of our family? Even before meeting Jeff, I was surrounded by the specter of a growing Orthodox community in my neighborhood. On Saturdays, when I'd drive along Olympic or Pico Boulevard on my way to shop or meet a friend for a movie, I'd see couples, families, and groups of friends dressed in their Shabbat finery, walking to or from shul. Sometimes I'd go to shul in the mornings at an egalitarian minyan where some of the women wore kippahs, as traditional men always would in shul. I was fine with checking in with my tribe on the occasional Saturday morning, as if I were popping a weekly spiritual vitamin, before dashing off for the rest of the day's shopping, dining, or writing. Yet part of me felt guilty when I drove past these religiously observant Jews, and I slunk a bit lower behind the steering wheel.

I was wrestling with the hardest decision in my life: whether to reach where no feminist Berkeley graduate that I knew of had gone before and take a deep dive into Orthodox teachings. I feared that even if it all went swimmingly (though in a more modest bathing suit), I would lose my friends—wonderful, caring, secular Jews with whom I had always shared left-of-center political and social views. If I headed rightward religiously while they stayed left, no amount of recycling or marching at women's rights rallies could compensate for that betrayal. Exposure to biblically based teachings helped me understand the conservative point of view more clearly. Discussions (okay, arguments) with Jeff over certain issues made me realize I had only heard one side of the story and that the views I had never considered before had merit.

In small incremental steps, I had already begun to feel some of my political views shifting toward more traditional ones, based on new teachings, philosophies, and documented historical patterns that pointed to their "rightness," morally, ethically, sociologically, and psychologically. This shift scared me, threatening my sense of self as a thoughtful, sophisticated, compassionate liberal. But what could I do? I couldn't clamp my hands over my ears and refuse to listen to these new ideas. I dreaded the prospect that a slowly growing philosophical chasm would open up between my friends and me, our years-long intimacy fracturing, possibly ending. Anticipating these losses made me almost unutterably sad.

My self-assessment was no fun at all and much more arduous than earning a master's in journalism. Trying to define myself relative to my Judaism loomed over me throughout the year, and there were no easy answers. But truth and eternity loomed, so I persevered.

The Community and the Corporation

*When your values are clear to you,
making decisions becomes easier.*
—Roy E. Disney

After finishing grad school, I returned to Los Angeles, and Jeff and I hit a rocky patch. I went with him regularly to Torah classes and occasionally to Shabbat meals. My earlier resistance was crumbling in the face of the truth and beauty in the lives I saw people living in the Venice community. While nothing is perfect and I knew perfectly well that what you can see from the outside often hides what may be going on inside, marriages and families around us appeared loving, respectful, and joyful—factoring in the normal chaos of life with children. These were people working to build wholesome, optimistic, enriched Jewish lives. This now seemed very attractive, and I wanted in. Looking at the society around me, I couldn't see how we could raise kids in a spiritually healthy way given the relentless, withering onslaught of secularism and materialism. I saw that we needed—that I needed—grounding in transcendent Jewish values. And yet, inner panic was growing, and I couldn't control it. One night, in emotional turmoil, I told Jeff that I couldn't go through with his Great Big Orthodox Adventure.

"I can't hold you back from living the life you envision for yourself. It's not fair to you or to me." Through my tears, I spoke to Jeff in the small den at my parents' condo where I was still living. "You deserve someone who won't keep battling you on this. You deserve someone who is all in just as you are."

Jeff left soon after my little speech, extremely upset. Early the next morning, he called. "We are not breaking up," he said, his voice ragged with emotion. I began to cry with relief. As soon as I had broken up with him I regretted it. Both of us had been up all night, sick with a feeling of loss. Was I really going to give up this wonderful, kind, funny, handsome man who celebrated my writing achievements, who was so proud of me, who told me I was beautiful, and who put up with my constant religious arguments, answering me patiently and with respect? Was I really going to give him up for Anna's *treyf* lasagna? Or shopping on Saturdays? What was I, meshugga?

We had a good thing going together and we both knew it. We came to an understanding that, once we married, we would keep baseline standards of observance of Shabbat and holidays, kashruth, and *taharat hamishpacha*, which govern intimate relations between husband and wife. I had been up in arms over that one for a long time, believing it sexist and anti-feminist. After finally reading about its purpose, source, and deeper meaning, it began to look quite different to me. Not easy to keep, but something that was designed to add spiritual integrity to our marriage and ultimately, build greater emotional intimacy. Jeff assured me I would go at my own pace for other mitzvah observances, such as choosing to cover my hair or not. Fat chance, I told him.

The following summer, a full year after my return from Washington DC, we married and moved into a shoebox-sized condo in Venice, where Jeff had been so warmly welcomed during the previous two years. Now I was embraced with equal enthusiasm. There were several other writers in this small, thriving community who all surpassed me in professional experience and reputation. I felt honored to be in their company.

Nearly to a person, we were *baalei teshuva*, boldly going back to the traditions of our ancestors. The term literally means "masters of return," but we knew we were far from being masters of Torah observance or knowledge. We all began as neophytes, finding our way back to our spiritual roots and our truest selves. Virtually none of our parents or siblings shared our journey, which led to friction between us and our family members, many of whom were disbelieving or antagonistic about our transitions. In typical Jewish fashion, they didn't hold back from letting us know they thought we had lost it, but this only strengthened our psychological ties to one another. We felt like a band of brothers and sisters, exploring our new yet ageless lifestyle.

Despite my earlier misgivings about "going Orthodox," I was very happy in my new life right from the start. Outwardly, nothing much had changed. I had a corporate job, and my wardrobe of skirts and dresses replaced the pants I had favored before. Jeff was no longer willing to eat at nonkosher restaurants, but I'd occasionally have vegetarian meals at nonkosher ones, either with girlfriends or with colleagues at work. We became friends with other young couples, including several who had also gotten married very recently. We enjoyed our weekly Torah classes and making special plans for Shabbat, inviting guests to our ministarter home or accepting invitations out. As young newlyweds committed to reigniting our Jewish roots, life felt expansive and full of promise.

The boundaries of a Torah-observant Jewish life felt practical as well as spiritual. We both tended toward workaholism, and Shabbat literally means "stop." What a great idea by God to mandate one day a week when we are redirected away from our endless quest for material achievements or conquests and urged instead to focus on the spiritual gifts that are ours for the taking! I did not yet pray regularly during the week, so the open space in time to go to shul and pray with my community became a meaningful, even emotional, experience.

Slowly, I learned the Shabbat liturgy that I had skimmed for so many years, having never paid close attention to the words and having never been taught it anyway. The words, the music, and our communal voices lifted in prayer struck me with a sense of poignant transcendence. My gratitude for having joined this community of people who were reclaiming our traditions grew daily. I believe I had always known at some subconscious level that the Torah really is a "tree of life" whose branches offer the best possible paths to wisdom, moral clarity, community, and peace. A purposeful life.

This commitment to Shabbat explains why, on a Friday afternoon, I was obsessively watching the clock at work. I was the publications editor in the Corporate Communications department of a *Fortune* 500 healthcare company, a plum position that I started just days before our wedding. The job opening had been whispered in my ear by a former colleague from UCLA who now had the office next to mine. Both of us enjoyed views of the city from our window walls on the seventh floor of our Wilshire Boulevard building in West Los Angeles.

I managed two publications: a monthly newsletter for the seventy thousand employees working in our acute rehab and psychiatric hospitals worldwide and a quarterly magazine for nurses in our acute care hospitals. Occasionally I drafted speeches for executives and polished their messages for employee newsletters. It was a cushy corporate environment and I liked it. On my first day I was handed a company-issued American Express card and a stack of personalized business cards. I freely charged business lunches, shared a secretary with a department colleague, hired freelance writers and photographers, and had travel arrangements made for me when I needed to attend meetings out of town. What a great gig!

When I was offered the job, I nervously showed my future boss, Tony, a list of the days I'd need off for religious holidays, plus the nonnegotiable condition about ducking out early on Fridays. In December, when sundown can be as early as 4:30 p.m., I'd need to leave by 2 p.m., but I assured him that I'd make up for any work time necessary by staying late on other days. Fortunately, Tony was a religious Catholic who kept a card of Saint Jude, patron saint of lost or impossible causes, peeking out of his shirt pocket every day. He was on board.

But that fateful Friday an earthquake had rumbled through a small town in northern California, damaging one of our hospitals. In situations like this, media relations departments like ours start revving their engines. This temblor was relatively minor and unlikely to make the national news. Injuries were few and fortunately there was no loss of life. Still, many patients needed to be evacuated to other facilities—and there weren't a whole lot of them in this remote area. In the Corporate Communications department, the honchos worried that the earthquake would thrust the company into the public eye. Members of the media, company shareholders, and state politicians would be watching to see how leadership managed it.

Frankly, I didn't see why this should affect me at all. I had plenty of time to report this story (and how remarkably capable everyone in the hospital had been in taking care of the patients) before my next newsletter deadline. But when I poked my head into Tony's office to say goodbye for the weekend, his expression was even more startled than usual. His eyes naturally bulged out beneath his dark, bushy eyebrows, giving him the permanent appearance of having suddenly stumbled across a crime scene.

"What? You can't leave now! We may need you to draft a statement for the media," Tony said.

This surprised me, as time-sensitive media releases weren't even part of my job. Besides, Tony was a seasoned PR guy twenty years my senior. He should have been able to rustle up an itty-bitty media release in his sleep.

But Tony knew I was a team player and hard worker and had proved it during my first several months on the job. For starters, I had begun to reverse the embarrassing slide in the monthly newsletter's production schedule, which had slipped badly under the dozing tenure of the previous editor. Tightening editorial and production deadlines,

I was pulling ahead a few days each month. Within six months I'd have my newsletter in readers' hands at the very beginning of its publication month—not at the end. I had also taken on an exciting design makeover of both my publications. Still, no earthquake-related media release could override my commitment to Shabbat.

"Tony," I said, "if there's anything I can do for you now, I can stay another twenty minutes, but that's really the absolute latest." He grudgingly allowed me to leave, though I did so with trepidation. The company was happy with me so far, and I didn't want my religious observance clouding my reputation. Tony was a good guy overall, sincere and well-intentioned, just prone to nervousness. His religious convictions made him a cheerleader over my new marriage. In fact, during my first few weeks on the job he'd often greet me in the morning with a sly smile and an exaggerated, "Good morning, *Mrs.* Gruen!"

My one big problem with Tony was the gag order he imposed over certain words in published copy, such as the word *said*. As a result, in the articles and interviews I published in my newsletters no one was ever quoted in the typical style, such as, "'We expect the new facility to open on March 10,' Mr. Zober said." Under Tony's editorial edict, people I quoted *recalled, observed, explained, acknowledged, commented, hoped,* or *reflected*, but never, ever *said*. Since this was all corporate communications, no one ever *kvetched, slammed, complained, seethed, huffed, accused,* or *groused*. Sometimes I fantasized about how grand and colorful my arsenal of quoting words would have been had I worked for some sort of whistleblower organization.

Tony further cramped my style by also banning the words *is* and *are*. These are rather handy verbs that one fails to appreciate fully until they have been imprisoned in the frozen language gulag where offensive verbs are sent to starve from neglect. A colleague had forewarned me about Tony's *mishigas*, so when he personally revealed these rules to me, I nodded with fake enthusiasm, trying to con him into believing I shared his zeal to root out passive voice and build an impenetrable wall under or over which the words *is* or *are* could not slink. Often, bumping verbs ahead to the lead of a sentence usually corrected issues of passive voice and made for more robust writing. But I soon found that sometimes, no matter how many ways I redesigned a sentence, nothing was as accurate as these mighty little verbs. My track record of close to 100 percent compliance would, I hoped, soften Tony's heart when he'd encounter the rare instance of the ghastly forms of the verb *to be*. No dice. My boss's red line was as literal as it was metaphorical. He'd toss the copy back on my desk, the verboten verbs circled in aggressive red strokes.

Tony's rigidity really began to stick in my craw, especially when I joined the great sisterhood of women enduring morning sickness during the early stages of pregnancy. "Morning sickness" seemed a real misnomer because pregnancy nausea doesn't arrive promptly at 7 a.m. and leave politely by noon. Nauseated and fatigued, my patience for Tony's rules began to fray. One afternoon, reeling because I smelled something metallic and horrid *all the time* that existed nowhere else outside my nose, and facing another accusatory red circle over a completely justified usage of "are," I stormed Tony's executive citadel.

I knocked but didn't even wait for him to say, "Come in!" I stood before him ready to combust. I tossed his edited copy back at him, a raging bull charging at the red ink.

"Tony, you know I'm doing good work here, but not everything is a 'reflection' or a 'representation' of something else." Slowing my pace as if speaking to the mentally deficient, I added, "Some things just *are*." I tried to make the word *are* sound like "ROAR!"

Seeing the look of terror on my boss's face, I basked in the glow of having ambushed him and the added feeling of power because I was standing, and he was sitting. "And another thing, Tony," I said, winding up for my final pitch, "I can't take this stress because I'm *pregnant*."

I waited as this news sank in, watching those protuberant eyes in fascination. If they swelled any further, I'd need to call an ambulance to take him to our nearest hospital.

"Oh! Okay. I'm sorry," Tony conceded. (Or possibly: *declared, admitted, sighed, mewled, surrendered, capitulated, forfeited, confessed*.)

I know; my attack on Tony was sneaky and a little mean. However, pregnancy offered the perfect excuse for an exercise in emotionally overwrought behavior. Why not use the power while I could wield it with impunity? I also knew that my outburst would—at most—buy me a few weeks of respite. Tony would revert to Helvetica type, and I'd have no choice but to adhere to his neurotic rules, even at the cost of clearer, cleaner copy.

As my due date neared, I had mixed feelings about leaving my job and handing it over to my replacement, Patty. Jeff and I had agreed that unless we had no choice, I would work part-time while our children were young. This was a shared priority, and I hadn't changed my mind, but the reality hit: I would really miss this job. True, this was PR, and the stories I wrote were cherry-picked to put my employer in a good light. I'm sure there were plenty of unsavory things roiling under the radar in our hospitals and rehab centers, but there were many feel-good stories that earned the attention we provided. One of my favorite stories—which I put on the cover of one newsletter—featured my interview with Sam Clover, a six-foot, three-inch Black RN and Air Force veteran. Known as the "gentle giant" in the psychiatric hospital where he cared for children traumatized by abuse, Sam's wisdom and dedication were poignant, and male nurses—let alone Black Air Force veteran RNs—were still very much an anomaly in the late 1980s.

I considered it a value to publicize these stories, giving employees reasons to feel proud of the company where they worked and spreading knowledge about leading-edge programs in health care. These included writing about the company's first facility designed for the specific needs of Alzheimer's patients, including a large circular path where patients could walk safely and freely on facility grounds. I interviewed a quadriplegic artist who had learned to paint through a company-sponsored program and stared in rapt fascination as he made fine brush strokes on paper with a small paintbrush he held in his mouth. I wrote about new trends and successes in specialty areas, such as thanatology, bariatric medicine, and rehab care of brain injuries. This work was immensely satisfying.

Nor had I lost the thrill of planning, writing, and overseeing the design of my publications. When the stacks of new newsletters arrived, I pulled one out and held it close, almost smelling the fresh ink, then held it at arm's length to evaluate how well the cover image looked. I was grateful for my talented bench of photographers, freelance writers, and our designer. I worried: If I stayed out of the corporate world for several years, how marketable would I be when I was ready to step back in? How would I keep up with new developments in technology, editorial style, and other changes?

Perilously close to my due date, my redesigned newsletter won first prize in its category at an awards ceremony for public relations professionals. My colleagues clapped as I waddled from my table in my peach-colored dress, and I collected my etched trophy. The awards dinner took place on the *Queen Mary*, which I found hilarious since by that point I felt nearly as vast as the cruise ship itself.

A few days later I packed up my office belongings, including my trophy. I welcomed my replacement, Patty, to my old office and her new one. I had liked Patty best among all the applicants I vetted and was pleased that Tony had hired her. She was also young, living with a screenwriter boyfriend about to hit it big with a blockbuster romantic comedy. She turned down my last-minute desperate request to consider job-sharing with me but gladly fed me steady assignments in my new role as a freelancer.

When I went into labor, I was sitting at my kitchen table, copyediting a newsletter for radio talk-show host and author Dennis Prager. The contractions soon became too intense for me to continue the work with any integrity, and I called Dennis to tell him of my condition. I apologized for not being able to finish the job.

"Do you think you could take it to the hospital with you?" he asked, hope in his voice. Clearly, he had never been in labor.

After the next set of contractions, I laughed. But it felt good to be asked.

Writing Against the Societal Tides

Sometimes the strength of motherhood is greater than natural laws.
—Barbara Kingsolver

"Mom bats the ball. See it go!" My five-year-old son, Avi, read from *Clifford at Bat*. His four-year-old brother, Noah, sat next to us, staring at the page with wide-eyed attention. As early as ten months old, Noah would crawl across the floor, dragging a book. When he reached me he'd lift the book up like an offering.

As a mother, I was naturally thrilled with Avi's budding literacy. As a mother and a writer, I savored the delicious anticipation that this son and all my children would always find as much pleasure in the world of reading as I did. My available time to read for pleasure was tightly constrained—at this point, I had three sons under six years of age and freelanced as a writer and editor. Still, I loved every moment I spent reading to my boys from our growing collection of children's books. We loved *The Runaway Bunny, Paddington*, and Mercer Mayer's charming "Little Critter" books, such as *Just Me and My Mom* and *All by Myself*. As Avi rapidly collected siblings, the pages of some of these books, particularly *The New Baby* and, perhaps not coincidentally, *I Was So Mad,* really took a beating.

As Avi's reading level steadily climbed from the first halting efforts to sound out words to a budding confidence and fluency, he was eager to read whatever he could, including simple, saucy media messages. Driving in the neighborhood one day, a billboard caught his attention. Miller's Outpost, at the time a popular clothing chain, splashed the image of a sexy woman clad in a tight-fitting pair of jeans, the zipper halfway undone, revealing an expanse of her sleek, bare abdomen. Maybe the photographer showed up before she had time to throw on a T-shirt?

"Get your butt in here!" Avi read the caption with a hint of naughty delight. In our family, we didn't consider the word "butt" a bad word, but when referring to our backsides, we used words like "behind" or "tushy," which felt a step up in class. Nuances in language mattered to us. We didn't allow the children to call one another "stupid" or tell one another to "shut up," wanting to instill in them the value that words do matter. Why not set the bar high at the beginning?

Confession is good for the soul, so I admit that when driving alone, I'd blast my favorite rock and roll music nearly at rock concert decibel levels. I wouldn't want my kids to hear most of this, at least not for many years, but for me it was an essential, slightly guilty indulgence. It was chocolate for this woman's late 1970s soul. Listening to the steady, heady doses of the music I loved evoked powerful emotions from my youth which fed my soul. I didn't even mind the sordid themes in some of the songs as much as the lyrics studded with grammar fails. (Maybe bad grammar had been locked and loaded into rock because it's so much easier to rhyme "ain't" than "isn't" and "done" than "doesn't.")

Back to my story. Mild as it was, the billboard was crude, sexually exploitative, and struck a blow against my children's innocence. With every passing season, the cultural arbiters and media mavens grew bolder in declaring foundational values—such as traditional marriage and God-based faith—irrelevant throwbacks to a hopelessly prudish and repressive past. This trend included imposing more adult messages and images in public, where young children could see them. It was a trend that had begun many decades earlier, but the pace was quickening.

Avi was too young to understand what the ad was really selling, and as parents, we had a short window in which to control the input of media messages, at least those that we could filter on our own. In a few scant years our kids would see and hear content through media channels and through other kids that we would not be aware of or control, content that could frighten, confuse, or disturb them. Billboards, music, movies, TV shows, video games, magazines, and books—even children's books—continued to parade overt sexuality of increasing varieties, emotional dysfunction, violence, and other content that was unhealthy for young children. As a mother, I was bound and determined to protect my children's innocence as long as possible—which wasn't long.

My own exposure to news media from the late 1960s, when I was a young child and voracious reader, had made me feel very insecure. Daily dispatches from the Vietnam War; violent student uprisings; race riots; the famous and the unknown overdosing on LSD and other drugs; and the assassinations of Martin Luther King and Robert Kennedy left me lying in bed awake at night, hearing the whirring of helicopters that increasingly hovered over our changing middle-class neighborhood. The neighborhood was changing, and not for the better. If I could do better for my own kids, I would.

The next day, I flipped through the mail only to see a postcard addressed to "resident" with the exact same billboard ad in miniature. Though easily discarded, the postcard angered me. A billboard claimed public space; this advertiser had invaded my private one. I found the phone number of the retailer's corporate office and asked to speak to someone in charge of regional advertising. To my surprise, I was quickly connected.

"The sexual message on the billboard was inappropriate enough," I explained, "but you had no right to send this to my house, my personal space. You've definitely lost me as a customer." The man listened politely and promised to discuss this campaign with colleagues. To my relief, the billboard came down soon after, though

I don't know what ultimately made it disappear.

My frustration at what I felt our declining culture was doing to hurt children's innocence had a positive flip side: it handed me an untapped new arena for my writing. With my protectionist feelings on behalf of the children of America still sizzling, I wrote a column about the billboard saga and sold it to a regional parenting magazine, showing parents what they could do in a similar situation. Looking at the world through the eyes of my young, impressionable children propelled me to fight for their right to be shielded from the seamier side of life as long as was reasonable. Selling the essay felt like a victory because the editor's purchase affirmed that many other parents were likely to share my concerns about how our culture was desensitizing our children—and us.

Life's frustrations and upsets are always gifts to writers in their own way. A favorite joke of mine goes something like this: a woman shows up to her weekly writers' group and announces, "I have news. I'm getting divorced, my dog died, and I need a knee replacement." A man in the group glares at her and grumbles resentfully, "Some writers have all the luck."

My fight against offensive billboards continued. For years after this incident, whenever a particularly offensive advertisement blighted our local landscape, I'd call the outdoor media company that had leased the space and explain politely but firmly that the ads offended our community standards. Some of these images were staggeringly gross. One ad placed by a local rock station showed four men from the back, standing with legs slightly spread, in a position to urinate. While their jeans were still mercifully on, it was still repellant. Ads promoting horror shows such as Dexter became commonplace, blood dripping from daggers or bodily orifices. Several soft-porn images advertised so-called gentlemen's clubs. It staggered me that I actually had to explain why these were problematic in a family neighborhood.

But how much time could I devote to this campaign? Sometimes

I rallied neighbors and friends, encouraging them to call about a particular billboard, but as I feared, as the years went by those in charge of these decisions cared less and less about the values of traditionally minded people like us. I felt like Sisyphus, pushing that hopelessly heavy boulder up the mountain.

I couldn't stop the trajectory of our society, but I could use my writing to promote a kinder, gentler one for the sake of our children. As one example, I wrote about the work of The Parents Television Council (PTC), an organization pushing back against networks that were broadcasting salacious and violent content even during TV's evening "family hour."

Here's the irony: as a society we cared deeply about children's physical health—we were vigilant about bike helmets, exercise, limiting sugar, and teaching about "stranger danger." But outside of folks in conservative and religious circles or activist groups such as at the PTC, who was even thinking about our children's psychological and spiritual health? Who was thinking about the impact that raunchy, violent, and otherwise explicit material could have on their hearts and minds? Apparently, no one in Hollywood. A show called *AHHH! Real Monsters* featured a trio that included a demon elf, another who held his own eyeballs, and a third who looked like a Tim Burton creation with crazy eyes. They all went to monster school to learn how to scare humans. If your first grader had nightmares, you might have had Nickelodeon to thank.

As a young mother, my creative drive remained strong—but motherhood was time-sensitive. If I missed out on providing the nurturing, teaching, comforting, and presence that my children needed in these early years, there were no do-overs. I curtailed my writing time but keenly felt moments of professional envy. Paging through women's magazines, especially those targeted to young moms like me, I'd look at the editors' photos and see how young they looked. Sometimes I felt my lips harden in a line as I thought, *That could have been me in that photo. I could have written the editor's column and decided what was published in each issue.*

Those jealousy pangs were fleeting but admittedly frequent. Still, it would have been shallow and ungrateful for me to linger on the "what if?" questions because I was blessed—very blessed—to live a wonderful life. I had a happy marriage, meaningful work, a growing spiritual connection with my Judaism, and the friendship of smart, warm, funny women with whom I could push my stroller to the park. These friends had also left professions behind or at least gone part-time as they tended the gardens of their own growing families. Between thousands of interruptions from our kids requesting snacks or demanding justice after a sibling snatched a toy from their little hands, my friends and I enjoyed robust conversations about anything and everything in life, including what we were learning and discovering in our still-novel, Shabbat-observant lives.

As a freelance writer, I volunteered to write for our synagogue newsletter and crafted marketing copy for our small day school. I picked up well-paid healthcare writing assignments from former colleagues, too. Still, it became crystal clear that while my writing was a vehicle to make a positive impact on the world, my work as a mother had even greater consequences. Watching my children's intellectual, emotional, and spiritual development, I felt the awesomeness of this responsibility. How do you help mold a healthy, confident, morally, ethically, and spiritually robust human being? With a few parenting scenes gone wrong, you could do a lot of damage that could haunt a child for life. As parents we would never get everything right; nobody can. But we were giving it our all, weighing our words and actions as carefully as we could as the moments would allow.

We learned from watching how our more experienced friends managed various child-rearing conundrums, as well as from the Torah's own lessons. Fratricide in the very first family on Earth? If Adam and Eve couldn't manage to control the squabbles between Cain and Abel, then we wouldn't sweat the frequent bickering over toys or sharing with friends. Giving a fancy embroidered coat to one child but nothing comparable for the rest? Trouble ahead! Daring to intervene in the expected path of inheritance by pushing the younger but worthier heir to the top leadership role? Dangerous but necessary. Couples disagreeing over their children's true character and future roles in the family? The mother is just about always right.

I was astonished to discover the poignant humanity of our matriarchs and patriarchs: the anguished infertility trials of Sarah, Rebecca, Rachel, and Hannah. The well-intentioned but disastrous displays of favoritism by Jacob to Joseph. Sarah's insistence that Ishmael, Abraham's first son, presented a clear and present danger to their son, Isaac, and had to be sent away. Rebecca's insight that younger twin Jacob, not Esau, deserved the blessing of the firstborn from their elderly father, Isaac, and her bold assumption of authority in making sure it turned out that way.

I hoped we would never encounter drama anywhere near these biblical proportions as we raised our own brood and felt increasingly thankful that I had bet on this life of "rules, rituals, and restraints" that Rabbi Daniel Lapin taught. The impact of what I was learning and living would add depth and substance to my work—because it's impossible to separate writing from life. The lessons I was absorbing into my consciousness would also affect our children, cascading through them and through their descendants.

My Fifteen Minutes of Writing About Fame

Careers are a jungle gym, not a ladder.
—Sheryl Sandberg

Last month Hollywood mourned the death of screen legend Gene Kelly, who died February 2 in his sleep at the age of 83. . . . I was engrossed in writing an obituary of the legendary Kelly for a Hollywood industry publication when my office phone rang.

"Judy? The kids have been waiting for you to pick them up," the school secretary said. "They said it was your day for carpool. Did you forget?"

A frisson of shock went through me. Sitting in my sixth-floor office in midtown Los Angeles, the secretary's call stunned me into realizing that in fact I had completely, totally, and without precedent forgotten to pick up my children and the two others in my carpool. The school was in Venice, two minutes from our home but a thirty-five to forty-minute drive from the office. I apologized to both the school secretary and my carpool partner, who was fortuitously available to dash out and collect our collective children. My capable housekeeper was already in charge of my two-year-old and four-year-old in the house. I could trust her to also deal with the six- and eight-year-olds as well until I arrived. I looked at the clock—how had it gotten so late?

What kind of mother forgets to pick up her own children? Fathers sometimes did, I realized. Jeff once returned home on a

Friday night after shul one child short of the two he had taken with him an hour and a half earlier. As he sauntered up to the front porch, I looked behind him into the dark night. "Where's Yael?" I asked. His face blanched. Then mine blanched, too. He pivoted on his heel and began running as fast as he had during his days on the high school track team. He began tearing down the sidewalk when our good friend Alan, a neighbor and the father of one of Yael's little friends, returned our daughter to us. Yes, it takes a village to raise—and not lose track of—children. "Don't worry," Alan said reassuringly. "I've done it too. But you can only do it once." He smiled knowingly and walked home with his daughters.

Working at this little magazine was a temporary gig, but I became possessive of the role mighty fast. I'd been freelancing for eight years, satisfied to juggle motherhood and work. I couldn't have done it without full-time household help, and I couldn't have afforded that without Jeff's hard work and success in running a small digital graphics and signage business. Many of my friends had jobs that didn't translate well to part-time or freelance work, and I considered myself fortunate.

My friend Sonia was the editor in chief of the magazine, and she had asked me if I wanted to fill in as the editor of one of the departments while she searched for a permanent hire. I didn't follow Hollywood news much, but the prospect excited me. It seemed like fun, and I wanted to prove that I could still blend seamlessly into an office environment and manage the editorial flow. Normally, I worked at a tiny computer desk in a corner of my living room, frequently interrupted by the urgent need to help build Duplo structures, mediate arguments over the ownership of yo-yos or other toys or cut up apple slices on command. At an office I would be free of these distractions and possible embarrassments.

Once, I had been on the phone trying to close a sale of my editing services to a new client. Unbeknownst to the client, I had a six-month-old baby clasped on my left hip during the entire call. She had been blissfully silent until suddenly she unleashed a thunderous belch into the receiver. I offered a nervous explanation of the circumstances, hoping the prospect didn't think I was a lush. He didn't hire me.

Preparing to return to the land of real, live office workers, I searched in the hinterlands of my closet, blowing the cobwebs off my professional wardrobe. Looking at a favorite skirt, I asked myself, "But will it still zip?" After four pregnancies, there were only so many weekly sessions of aerobics and Pilates I was willing to endure for the futile goal of recapturing my long-lost waist. That was a satisfying little feature while it lasted, and I missed cinching those belts just so. I worried that everyone else at the magazine would be dressed with trendy Hollywood flair, while I showed up in dated and slightly musty work outfits. I dreaded having my clothing mark me as some dowdy momma in Tinseltown.

This was not my only concern. What if someone in the break room asked my opinion of some of the latest movies, such as *Leaving Las Vegas* or *The Quick and the Dead*? Most of the films I saw those days were animated productions starring talking animals, so in case of such an emergency, I'd have to pour my coffee fast and race back to my office. However, if anyone wanted my opinion about *Babe*, *Toy Story* or *The Lion King*, I'd be on it like whipped cream on a sundae.

That afternoon when I forgot about my kids, I was jolted into realizing how much of my sense of self and even my sense of worth was bonded to my writing. That's why I could so easily become engrossed in my work, even forgetting I had children while I joyously ruminated over word choices: Should it be *dismayed* or *distraught*? How about *perturbed*? Would *discomposed* sound too Victorian? Time really flies when luxuriating over the 1,300-plus pages of a *Roget's Thesaurus*. When one of my sons had first heard me mention the name of this beloved writing accessory, he asked, "Is that a kind of dinosaur?"

In general, I made no apologies for my intensity at work, but as my friend Denise pointed out, "Your dinners are paying the ultimate price." I burned endless pots of rice while riveted to my computer screen, recrafting sentences, redesigning the architecture of paragraphs, constantly asking myself: how can I improve this? Why hadn't anyone told me about the marvelous invention of the rice cooker years earlier, especially my next-door neighbors, who undoubtedly smelled the charred grain at least once a week? Overall, I struggled to find the right balance between professionalism (aka meeting deadlines) and self-absorbed perfectionism.

My tenure as a magazine department editor was fleeting—even briefer than some Hollywood marriages. I was in the groove, enjoying the interviewing, writing, and editing, until one morning I arrived at work to learn that my services were no longer required. Walking into *my* office, I saw unfamiliar and creepy magazines fanned out along *my* little credenza next to *my* couch. In those days, my magazine taste ran to *Parents, Woman's Day*, and the *Washington Post Book Review*. The magazines sullying *my* credenza featured Goth-inspired models, their hairstyles aping the look of a set of Japanese chef knives. Their lips were glossed in black, their leather pants tight on their malnourished legs, and accessorized by chains that looked like they could anchor a cruise ship. Who had violated my space?

The redecorating mystery was solved within minutes when a woman several years younger than me sashayed into the office that I now understood was no longer mine. She was dressed as if she had tracked down the exact outfit worn on the cover of the January issue of *Creepster Magazine*.

She looked at me as if I were a lost tourist and asked, "Can I help you?"

"This is my office," I said with faux conviction.

"Oh, didn't Sonia tell you? I'm the new editor." She stood facing me with a hard look. I noticed that her hair was a shade of black that does not exist in the natural world. Before she had poured her first cup of coffee on the job, she had become even more territorial than I had. Was this a female thing, I wondered?

My education in Jewish values had taught me so much wisdom. This included giving other people the benefit of the doubt, greeting others with a smile, and treating others as you would want them to treat you. But at that moment, I just despised this woman—who was not much more than a kid—for her arrogance, her appalling lack of any grace, and her ghoulish black nail polish. Was that supposed to be attractive or a warning—like the skull-and-crossbones image on containers warning of poison inside?

"Well, this job must have been a real feather in your cap," she said condescendingly, as I felt a rising fury. I balled my hands into tight fists and worked my jaw hard to keep it from dropping to the floor. I didn't need my *Roget's Thesaurus* to summon a whole slew of salty words I wanted to spew at this interloper. Who did she think she was? Why did she assume I was playing dress-up editor?

And then it hit me. I considered the outfit I was wearing that day and what it must have telegraphed to her. She was dressed for barhopping on Melrose Avenue. But I was dressed like I was running a subscription drive for the *Saturday Evening Post*, and my shoes (oh, why had I worn *these* shoes today?) screamed "ARCH SUPPORT!" But why did I score no points for my chic beret? I often splurged on designer chapeaux to make the mitzvah of covering my hair easier. I know these hats flattered me and did me proud. But as these thoughts ran amok in my head, I began to feel something tickling my leg. Swiftly glancing down I saw that the hem of my skirt was coming undone. So much for a seamless reentry into the office work world. My skirt was unraveling and so was I.

"Actually, I have *many* years of experience in journalism and publications management," I parried. *Please don't notice my falling hem*, I prayed. "I'm going to find Sonia," I said, turning on my sensible low heel and away from this insufferable upstart.

But first I stopped at the secretary's desk, where I whispered a request for Scotch tape. Seeing my mortified expression, she handed it to me with a sympathetic nod. In the ladies' room, I taped the hem on my drab plaid skirt, which I would hurl into the Goodwill bag as soon as I got home.

I found Sonia and informed her that my replacement had just landed.

"Oh no! Judy, I can't believe I forgot to tell you," she said, looking genuinely abashed. "I am sorry—please forgive me. You know how crazy it's been around here with awards season and all. Everyone's having nervous breakdowns."

I assured her it was all right, but I was thinking: *Good luck. If you need another fill-in when this civility-challenged chick implodes, you've got my number.* In the parking lot, I headed toward my money pit of an old minivan just as I saw Jack Lemmon exiting his gray Rolls Royce. He was parked in a row reserved for cars that screamed, *I'm obscenely rich!*

My temporary job had ended with a crash landing, but I was still grateful to Sonia for the opportunity. Before the Mean Girl editor arrived, I had fun dipping my toe into Tinseltown, while also seeing that it would never have been a job that could have satisfied me on a long-term basis. My writing center of gravity lay outside that world. And I'd return to it now, thinking of ideas while waiting in the carpool line.

Author! Author!

You were born to win, but to be a winner, you must plan to win, prepare to win, and expect to win.
—Zig Ziglar

While waiting for the light to turn green at a busy intersection and innocently wondering what movies were playing at the Cineplex across the street, three little words suddenly dropped like creative pixie dust in my imagination. In that split second, I decided to write my first book.

Before I stopped at that red light, I had been a happy juggler: motherhood in both hands and freelance writing being tossed from left to right. I had no concepts for books floating around in my mind. None. But the phrase *carpool tunnel syndrome* had instantly become a force to be reckoned with. By the time the light changed and I hit the gas, ideas for funny stories about motherhood and family life tumbled over each other, like little kids scrambling around in one of those huge ball pits. How could I *not* write the book? A clever title is a terrible thing to waste.

Borrowing Bette Davis's famous adage that old age is no place for sissies, I already knew that the same held true for book publishing. I followed industry trends, read book reviews voraciously, and had many author friends. Writing a book would demand dedicated time and focused energy, but that would be the easy part.

As someone with minimal name recognition, I wasn't going to even bother trying to get an agent for my book. I knew it would sell very modestly, even under the best of circumstances. I would hunt for a small publisher that accepted unagented submissions, earn endorsements and positive reviews, gin up publicity, and pray for sales totaling more than, say, forty-three. I immersed myself deeply into the current realities of the book publishing world, and decided I could dive into self-publishing and self-promotion eagerly. I'd have to work very, very hard, especially in the months before publication because, bestsellers aside, most books sell virtually all of what they will ever sell during the first year after publication.

There were long odds against my success, but so what? I wouldn't let any of it stop me from reaching for my dream. I was raring to write, jazzed by my ideas, and wanted to share the gift of laughter—something everybody needs—*especially* parents raising kids who claim they cannot go to school because of ailments such as "itchy right eyebrow" and "fat hair." My kids, ranging in age from six to twelve, were bountiful founts of comedic material.

Chapters started writing themselves right away. "Tanks but No Tanks" chronicled our disastrous experiment in the maintenance of "free" goldfish in a costly tank that required all sorts of atmospheric necessities such as colorful gravel, water conditioner, plants ("for the ambiance," we were told), and a fish-friendly equivalent of Prozac to keep the fish calm. "Why Guar Gum Is Really a Vegetable" confessed the kind of dog-and-pony show I produced each night, trying to provide a balanced diet for children who would only eat foods that started with the letter P. Writing "The 700 Habits of Highly Defective Parents" probably saved me thousands in therapy dollars. It was cathartic to share all the parenting gimmicks that experts promised would work beautifully but were epic fails in real life. When I tried the scheme of "reflecting my children's feelings back to them," instead of falling into line behaviorally like the experts said they would, they just looked at me funny and asked, "You feeling okay, Mom?" and then resumed fighting.

Oh yes. I would do this. I set a goal to publish it within the year—when I would turn forty.

Erma Bombeck had been my writing heroine and mentor. Beginning at the age of eight I had snapped open the newspaper three times a week to delight in her hilarious columns. I read them again and again for sheer pleasure but began to absorb lessons in the art of humor writing at the same time. Everybody loved Erma's self-deprecating tone, which worked because her inner confidence also shone through. She could be edgy without ever crossing the line to cynicism or bitterness. Her sly, wry perspective on modern suburban marriage and motherhood was relatable and often side-splittingly funny. At the peak of her success, she was syndicated in more than seven hundred newspapers while also writing books, too, such as *If Life Is a Bowl of Cherries, What Am I Doing in the Pits?* I had wanted to be like Erma Bombeck when I grew up, only Jewish. When she died in 1996 from complications after a kidney transplant, I mourned her loss and even wrote a condolence letter to her family. I sensed that from her cushy abode in the A-list comedy section of Heaven she would cheer me on.

My family had grown accustomed to my stories about our family life appearing in print. The children were still young enough and their problems all still manageable enough that I could knead their antics, arguments, and absurdities into funny stories without damaging anyone's emotional stability. (I hoped.) Sometimes, it was enormously frustrating to watch so much hilarity playing out in front of my eyes but know I could never share it on the page. Family privacy demanded discretion, but as a writer, it was an appalling sacrifice of rich copy. I socked each episode away in a cerebral file drawer. When the time was right, one day I would shine daylight on them—though probably in a novel.

Self-publishing was a fast-growing trend, but self-published books were still sneered at by virtually everybody associated with the traditional publishing field. They were not eligible for reviews in important book industry journals, and faced long odds of getting distributed through Ingram, the powerhouse book distribution channel for bookstores and some libraries. If a book wasn't in Ingram's system, almost no bookstores would ever know about it or order it. Until that time, around 2001, most self-published books were produced by "vanity" presses that did no vetting of the material. Any junk slapped between two book covers could get published. Even with scores of reputable self-publishing companies and indie publishers elevating the industry by having a manuscript review process, most people considered any self-published book a vanity project that all but screamed, "I COULDN'T GET A REAL PUBLISHER!"

The fast-growing world of self-publishing opened up my options considerably. Not only did I decide to shrug off the prejudice against it but comforted myself with the long list of well-known authors who also failed to entice a traditional publisher and self-published: St. Louis homemaker Irma S. Rombauer privately printed 3,000 copies of *The Joy of Cooking* before it got picked up by Bobbs-Merrill Company and went on to sell more than 18 million copies. Marcel Proust paid to publish 1,000 copies of *Swann's Way*, the first volume of his seven-volume novel series, *Remembrance of Things Past*. Beatrix Potter self-published 250 copies of *The Tale of Peter Rabbit* after she tired of collecting rejection notices. Within a year, one of the publishers who had refused it picked it up and sold 20,000 copies right away. Over 2 million Beatrix Potter books are sold each year. Poet E. E. Cummings published a collection of poetry called *No Thanks,* the title a cheeky nod to the fourteen publishing houses that had refused the collection; W. W. Norton and Company eventually published it. Modern-day examples include Dr. Wayne Dyer's *Your Erroneous Zones;* Richard N. Bolles's *What Color Is Your Parachute?;* Christopher Paolini's *Eragon* fantasy series for young adults; and Margaret Atwood's poetry collection, *Double Persephone* (this was before she wrote her blockbuster novel *The Handmaid's Tale).*

I submitted *Carpool Tunnel Syndrome: Motherhood as Shuttle Diplomacy* to a publisher in Northern California who had encouraged me to send it her way. I tenderly swaddled my typed, bound manuscript in a secure box and said a little prayer as I handed it over to the clerk at FedEx, who put it into the mysterious back room where FedEx packages begin their journeys. A few weeks later, she sent me a gracious note complimenting my writing but rejecting the submission as not a good fit for her list. Given the long odds, I was not surprised, though I felt sorely disappointed.

Shortly after, a friend convinced me to publish my book under her new fledgling publishing company. Doing business with a friend is always risky, but she was a talented graphic designer and was already going to publish her husband's book. Despite misgivings, I agreed. "Lisa" and I had worked together in the past, and she was very smart, skilled, organized, and honest. However, she could also be very headstrong, so I made it clear that all final editorial decisions would be mine and mine alone. I knew that Lisa's design skills would ensure my book looked professional, light-years ahead of the embarrassing, amateurish look that still marked too many self-published books and made it a heavy lift for this category of publishing to gain respect. In working with Lisa, I could also get my book out by my target date; no waiting for twelve or eighteen months to fit into a standard publisher's production schedule.

Lisa did a fantastic job designing the book, both the interior pages and the cover. She offered sound editing advice—which I heeded—and got my book into the Ingram distribution system. I hired cartoonist John Caldwell, whose work I had long admired, to draw the cover image. I hustled for endorsements from parenting and book review sites as well as bigger catches, including *Los Angeles Times* columnist Chris Erskine, and Bil Keane, creator of *The Family Circus*, whose cartoons graced the covers of several of Erma Bombeck's books. *I was thrilled with Keane's generous quote:* "While my cartoons are a quick take on typical family life, Judy Gruen picks up where I left off. I thank the Good Lord she's not drawing a newspaper comic. Get into this carpool. You'll enjoy the ride." *I ended up with eleven strong endorsements that greeted readers on the first inside pages.*

Still, I had read the tea leaves correctly. Writing my book was a cakewalk compared to the roller coaster experience of publishing and promotion. I devoured newsletters and books by John Kremer and Dan Poynter, experts on self-publishing and book promotion, and was pumped to work hard. From these sources I learned that Scholastic Book Fairs bought some books written for parents, and my pitch letter clinched a sale of 2,500 copies to sell at book fairs across the country. This was close to my entire first print run, and I was elated. My euphoria was tempered—but only slightly—when I received instructions to ship them in small to tiny quantities to more than one hundred addresses: four to a school in Podunk, Kansas; twelve to Smackover, Arkansas; eighteen to Sandwich, Illinois; thirty-two to Amityville, New York; and so on. I hired a high-school kid to help me pack, address, and ship the books. It was a full day's work to get it done, and despite the laboriousness of the effort, scoring a bulk sale remained a proud victory.

I sold an excerpt from my book to *Woman's Day* from my chapter called "Big-Food-A-Plenty," about the unexpected challenges of saving money by shopping at Costco:

> Wondering how to invigorate both my sagging assets and skin at the same time, I looked for money-saving ideas. I found that one of those member-only warehouse stores had opened up near me, so I ran right over and plunked down $40.00 for the privilege of pushing around a shopping cart the size of a tractor. Once inside Big Food-A-Plenty, I didn't know where to begin, but I had to think fast: a forklift was speeding my way, beeping threateningly. This was a supermarket on steroids, eight times larger than the Houston Astrodome, and there was nothing it didn't sell: pasta by the pound, socks by the scores, pickles in profusion. Whatever you wanted to buy at Big Food-A-Plenty, you had better like it, because it only came in multiples.

Woman's Day had a circulation of more than six million readers at the time, and Lisa and I were sure that this fabulous exposure would ensure book sales beyond my wildest dreams. I secured book signings at major bookstores including Barnes & Noble and Brentano's. So far, I felt totally vindicated in my decision to self-publish. Even without reviews in industry review journals, which refused self-published titles, my own grit and determination were paying off.

But great exposure didn't ensure any sort of commensurate sales boost. No sales boost was even detectable after the *Woman's Day* excerpt was published. A syndicated radio host with more than ten million listeners also promoted my book on her show, offering a free copy to the first three listeners who called into Lisa's 800 number, but Lisa's phone began ringing at six in the morning, hours before the show began locally, and continued incessantly until seven in the evening. The producer had failed to tell us that the show was broadcast in *many* different time zones all across the country. We were apologizing all day long and were pretty ticked off.

I bought a table at an outdoor Jewish community fair in June to sell my book. The agreement stated NO REFUNDS, EVEN IF IT RAINS. I laughed. Rain? In *June*? In *Southern California*? I mailed in my check. Under angry, gray skies I shlepped four cases to my table and placed several copies in brand new, clear Lucite book stands. The clouds burst open, sending sheets of rain over my inventory. I raced back to my car with case after case of books. However, other vendors were sticking around, the rain began to ease, and to pass the time I visited another vendor and bought a beautiful, wildly impractical beaded evening bag. After six miserable hours, the vendors began packing up. I had not sold a single book and felt humiliated. But then, a vision! I recognized a man I had met years before through a camp where we both had worked.

"Phil? Is that you?" I rushed the guy and shamelessly, piteously begged him to buy a book. To stop my groveling, he did.

It began to rain again steadily on the long drive home. When my six-year-old daughter called to ask how many books I had sold, I stupidly told her the truth.

"That's ALL?" she screamed. "Only ONE? MOMMY ONLY SOLD ONE BOOK AT THE FAIR!" she shouted to her brothers and father. Jeff performed an intervention and grabbed the phone, then offered much-needed comfort for my soggy misery.

I still had other irons in the fire. Coming up in early fall would be my first speaking event at the Jewish Federation Council in Los Angeles. After considering and rejecting several dates for the event, the organizer and I had settled on one that seemed to be perfect for everyone. They placed ads in the *Jewish Journal*, where I had some name recognition. I couldn't wait for this opportunity—my first book event at a significant venue.

I marked my calendar for the special night: September 11, 2001.

Crises

There is a thin line that separates laughter and pain, comedy and tragedy, humor and hurt.
—Erma Bombeck

Many authors deflate emotionally after their books are published. This is normal, the literary equivalent of a mild post-partum depression. After all the tireless work invested, the anticipation, and the excitement, the success of the book is simply out of your control. *Carpool Tunnel Syndrome*'s launch had been respectable, and I had a lot to be proud of. But in short order, I faced two personal crises that underscored this comedown.

For one thing, my mother had been unwell for many weeks, my worry ballooning into intense anxiety. While under a doctor's care she continued to worsen, and I was becoming frantic. By the time she was admitted to the emergency room a few months later and comprehensive tests were finally done, it was too late. Her cancer had metastasized so thoroughly that no one could even tell its point of origin. Her spectacularly incompetent doctor had missed all the classic symptoms. All he could say was, "It's a good time to gather the family around and look at family pictures together." Truly, if looks could kill, he would have been dead on that hospital floor.

I was enraged at the doctor, but I also blamed myself for not having intervened much earlier. I was wrapped up with my family and yes, with my book. It is something I have had to live with ever since. At the same time—because crises like to spontaneously replicate—

that unease I had felt from the beginning about my unusual and untested publishing arrangement with Lisa proved to be prophetic. Her marriage was unraveling in an ugly and volatile manner. She warned me that she didn't see how she could continue carrying out her agreed-upon role of managing book sales, distribution, accounting, and other administrative tasks. My job was pursuing marketing and special sales opportunities and shipping books to the distributor for every order. I spent a lot of time standing in line at the post office, balancing boxes in my arms.

I hoped and prayed that Lisa wouldn't bail. It's not as if my book was the latest Oprah pick selling by the tens of thousands. How much administrative work could there have been? But soon after, Lisa lowered the boom—she was shutting down her publishing company and declaring both titles she had just published out of print. This was a disaster. I begged her not to do this, offering to handle any and all work involved in keeping my title alive. Once a publisher declares a book out of print, all sales from within the major industry inventory system cease. The ISBN number can only be associated with one published version of a book. Mere months after its promising debut, my book would be pulled from the book distribution food chain. Lisa was killing my book.

I was reeling from this crushing double whammy. I was distraught over my mother's diagnosis, unable to imagine my life without her in it. Yet I was also furious at Lisa even as I sympathized with her crumbling family situation. I reminded myself daily that even if I had to publish my book all over again, my marriage (thank God) was rock solid and my family life intact. Nothing mattered more than that—except for my mother having incurable cancer.

I began to cry a lot. During walks together in the late afternoon or early evening, my husband would play therapist, listening as I regaled him with my publishing woes—not that he didn't already know them in great detail—while trying to help me figure out how to deal with Lisa and save my book. It was selling steadily, though in small numbers. I felt wronged, aggrieved, and foolish for not having listened to my intuition, or to Jeff, who had seen the red flags earlier and warned me against this venture. Could I even find another publisher to re-release it if its main sales strength had already waned? I had no choice but to search. I knew I was not suited to the administrative work involved in setting up my own publishing company, so at least I listened to that inner voice of truth.

My mother was naturally proud of me for my achievement of writing and publishing my first book. I was grateful that she lived to see it and *shep nachas*, take great pleasure, as we say in Yiddish. Naturally, I had dedicated the book to her. This is how the dedication read:

> *To my mother, Liebe Rosenfeld, who taught me from an early age that I could achieve whatever I set out to do. Her love, encouragement and strength continue to nourish me . . .*
>
> *And in memory of my mother-in-law, Laura Gruen, who passed away while I was writing this book. Her warmth and laughter are sorely missed.*

All I could do was to spend as much time with my mother as I could, and while she still felt reasonably well, she met me at a Chanukah boutique at a large, affluent synagogue where I had bought a table. Yes, this was after the unmitigated disaster of the rained-out outdoor fair where my only book sale resulted from abject begging. But *this* event, oh, this would be much different!

I was assured that this would be a great place to sell my book. Hundreds of women with gushing checking accounts and a spending problem would storm the battlements to shop till they dropped. They had even given me a table right outside the hall, just to the side of the entrance doors. Everybody would see me! Nobody could miss me! In another example of blind hope triumphing over cruel experience, I loaded my car with cases and cases of books. Who among these hundreds of Jewish women wouldn't want my book for Chanukah? Jews are known to be the people of the book, but it should be "books." Go to a Jewish house and see how many books are on the shelves. Naturally, these women would want one for themselves, and a few for their sisters, aunts, daughters, and friends!

I was well dressed, and my makeup looked good. Mom sat on a chair just a few feet away from me so that it didn't look like I had brought my mom along to my lemonade stand. (This was her idea to sit apart, not mine.) The women began surging in like a tidal wave as the doors opened. I had prepared a few greetings that I hoped would captivate shoppers.

"Hi there! Would you love to take home the gift of laughter?"—"Hi! Do your kids ever actually listen to what you say, the first time?" (I thought that would really be a showstopper.)—"Do you believe the government should pay for abdominal liposuction for America's mothers?" (I didn't actually say this. But might it have helped?)

The women charged by me like warriors. They were not interested in reading matter. They wanted Pashmina scarves. Handmade jewelry. Handbags of the softest pebbled leather. Boutique clothing. These shoppers were dropping thousands of greenbacks by the hour—inside the hall.

I greeted one woman I knew casually with a big smile. She had kids! I got her to physically pick up a book (halfway to a sale is when it's in the customer's hands, right?). She looked at it and said to me with a dour look, "I don't have a sense of humor." I glanced at my mom, who had a pained look on her face. I was forty years old, and my poor mother was watching me fail publicly at something where I had so wanted to shine, if only for her sake. One of the things that had always made her a great mom was that she never tried to protect me from life's skirmishes. She knew I was a scrapper and had learned to dust myself off after getting knocked down. This was the last time she would be with me at a professional event, and I couldn't give her the satisfaction of seeing me succeed. I felt worse for her than for me.

An early Chanukah miracle was that this boutique was not quite the utter humiliation of the outdoor festival. One case of books was noticeably lighter when I started loading the car up again after standing on my feet for seven hours. Despite the increased strength in my biceps, this event also cured me from ever, *ever, EVER* signing up for any sort of boutique or fair again, unless I went into the Pashmina shawl business. I finally learned that unless it was a book fair, even Jews didn't buy books at these events.

By the end of July, and just two weeks before my eldest son's bar mitzvah, Mom passed away. Lisa and I had resolved our dispute through a mediator, and I was shopping for a new publisher. I was jazzed for my big speaking event on Tuesday evening, September 11 at the Jewish Federation.

But when my radio went on that morning at 6:45 to my local NPR station, I realized there would be no speaking event that night. I had difficulty absorbing what the reporters and hosts were broadcasting. The Twin Towers were collapsing in fire, and two other commercial planes had also been hijacked and crashed: one into the west side of the Pentagon; the other, United Airlines flight 93, into a field near Shanksville, Pennsylvania after a few incredibly brave passengers fought to regain control of the aircraft and divert it from its intended target.

The reporters seemed to be speaking just a half beat slower than usual, an indication of their own shock. I didn't say anything to the children but got them ready for school as usual. Only when I drove up to their day school and saw the principal standing outside, telling parents there would be no school today, did the gravity of the situation begin to sink in. Of course there wouldn't be school today. Despite our being clear across the country from the attacks, how could I have thought anything would be normal that day?

That night, huddled in the living room and following the inexplicable news like everybody else in the nation, people began to wonder aloud about when and where further attacks would take place. With LA the center of the entertainment industry and home to hundreds of thousands of Jews, our city would make an enticing target for Muslim terrorists.

Jeff and I had long anticipated that the day might come when it would become dangerous for us to be identifiably Jewish in public here in the United States. This country had been very good to us, anti-Semitism notwithstanding. But even when we were dating, Jeff said that he didn't feel the good times would last for Jews in the US. He wasn't a pessimist by nature, but good times had not lasted for Jews anywhere in the diaspora throughout our long history. Our freedom was a double-edged sword, creating a "debilitating affluence," in the words of Rabbi Shimshon Raphael Hirsch. Similarly, Rabbi Chaim Volozhin (1749–1821) observed, "When Jews forget to make Kiddush, non-Jews will make Havdalah." Meaning: when Jews stop observing the Sabbath and our other sacred rituals, non-Jews will remind us of our outsider status through anti-Semitism.

Were these attacks now the tipping point? Jews in Israel already lived with the anxiety of waiting for the next Intifada or violent riot to explode. While I worried and prayed for the safety of my people in Israel, beginning that day murderous attacks were no longer "over there" in Israel and occasionally Europe and South America. Terrorism had hit us where we lived. Anti-Semites wouldn't care whether Jews were religious or not—Jew-hatred doesn't discriminate between the secular or the observant—but we were visibly religious. Jeff and our sons (once over the age of three) wore kippahs on their heads and the four-cornered white undershirt whose *tzitzit* strings dangled from the corners of their pants. (These could be tucked in, but no five-year-old can be bothered with this.) After we had been married for about four years, I began to cover my hair in public and had migrated my wardrobe to below-the-knee skirts and dresses with half- or three-quarter-inch sleeves. In a secular society where people seemed to wear beach clothes even in restaurants or in shopping malls, we definitely stood out as "other" and Jewish.

Almost immediately after the attacks, articles began questioning whether anything could be funny anymore. Many comedy clubs closed temporarily. One article announced, "Humor Goes into Hiding." The moment was raw, and our nation was traumatized, but of course humor and comedy would return—and soon—because it had to. Humor isn't a luxury; it's a survival tool. It releases anxieties from shared fears and concerns. It lets us laugh at the absurd, and even at evil. We need this.

Despite this strong belief, I couldn't help but fret that perhaps my humor writing was self-absorbed or just not as important as other writing I could do. In an age of terrorism, should I leave the humor to others and focus most of my efforts on serious topics, especially topics of relevance to Jewish life? I asked my trusted and wise rabbi his opinion.

"Absolutely not," Rabbi Moshe Cohen said. "We need to laugh now more than ever. Your work is important."

Affirmations that he was correct began trickling in. First was an email from a woman who had read my book excerpt in *Woman's Day* while in a doctor's waiting room. "I want you to know you saved my life today," she wrote. "I was so depressed by my medical condition that I wasn't sure I wanted to keep fighting. You made me laugh, and it made all the difference."

I was staggered. Her declaration that my light humor column had "saved her life" was a wild overstatement, but that was her perception, which became her reality. Then a casual friend in the market sidled over to me and said in a hushed tone, "I am *so* glad to know I am not the only one with an eleven-year-old who still eats with his hands!" She really was relieved!

I never again doubted that writing for laughs was in its own way, serious business.

Kosher Dilemmas

According to the effort is the reward.
—Ethics of the Fathers 5:26

Attending professional conferences presents challenges to Shabbat-observant Jews. Most are on the weekends, but unless the conference takes place in some wooded campground or a monastery, during Shabbat religiously observant Jews must navigate the obstacle course of the ubiquitous lights, door locks, toilet flushes, and entry doors that are all triggered electronically. Triggering any electronic circuit to go on or off during Shabbat violates one of the rules against creative actions during our day of rest. We let things be, having preset them as needed before Shabbat begins. So, no picking up our iPhones, computers, or lighting a match. They don't seem like "work," naturally, but they are all actions that express our agency in the world.

When I attended the Erma Bombeck Writers Conference in 2004 at Erma's alma mater, the University of Dayton, I faced down a few such challenges, including one to my reputation as a Shabbat-observant Jew. I'd been invited as a panel member, along with humor columnists Mickey Guisewite and Patricia Wynn Brown, to discuss the topic of finding humor in everyday life. The weekend conference was hosted every other year and dedicated to the business and craft of writing—humor writing in particular.

The main sessions would begin on Saturday, but on Friday night I was also invited to a dinner for conference speakers and VIPs, such as Bill Bombeck, Erma's widower, and their three children. I'm not sure how this happened but I was thrilled to have been seated next to Mr. Bombeck—a real honor. Among a handful of other conference speakers, I had been asked to say a few words to the group of about sixty about how Erma's work influenced me. My short, amusing remarks were all locked and loaded, ready to fire, but as I spied the microphone at the podium, I faced a quandary. Using a microphone was prohibited over Shabbat—what was I going to do when they called my name? While talking to Bill Bombeck I tried to think of a clever solution but kept drawing a blank. Thankfully, as I was introduced, Divine inspiration tapped me on the shoulder.

As everyone else had done, I first walked behind the podium as if positioning my short self to speak into the microphone. I waited just a second or two, looked at the audience and shrugged, then walked around to stand in front of the podium. "I've got four teenagers at home," I said with an exaggerated sigh. "I don't *need* a microphone," gesturing helplessly. The audience laughed appreciatively, and I was home free. *Great idea, God! Thank you!* I said to the Almighty.

At the large banquet the next night, I faced my most embarrassing situation as a kosher traveler among non-Jews. I was the only Orthodox Jew among the group of about 350 people, seated at one of the round banquet tables in the hall. As my congenial table mates were all enjoying their *treyf* dinners of warm rolls, baked chicken, whipped potatoes, and green beans almondine, I was busy trying to hack my way through the kosher meal specially ordered for me. The caterer had provided me with feeble plastic cutlery, but I needed a machete to slice through the dinner's suffocating layers of industrial-strength aluminum foil and two layers of building-grade plastic wrap. A few guests at the table stole furtive, sympathetic glances my way as I labored to excavate my dinner, trying to appear unflustered. *After all this work, it better be good,* I grumbled inwardly.

It was a multitasking ordeal. I chatted with my neighbors about column topics, submitting to syndicates, and dealing with rejection, while slashing and cutting with as much grace as I could muster. Even the stainless-steel knife that I picked up from my place setting seemed powerless against the kosher catering forces defending me from any contact with nonkosher comestibles. The waiter determinedly circled the table, trying to pour the nonkosher wine into the wineglass I shielded with my hand. I couldn't blame the guy. I'm sure I looked like I needed a drink. Probably two.

Truly, I was cringing inside. The caterer's overkill efforts in bundling this little dinner as if it were being loaded onto a NASA rocket into space were an embarrassment to me. This would never have happened in LA or any other more sophisticated Jewish community. I had full confidence in my religious identity, knowing that the Torah and its commandments "are our life and the length of our days." I gladly stood out by sporting hair coverings and outfits with more discreet dimensions than most women wore. The Catholic university was very helpful in arranging a campus escort to walk me in the evenings to the home where I was being hosted by a Jewish family, about a mile away from the campus. But I simply hated for people to think that my Jewishly committed lifestyle—keeping kosher in particular—was such a burden, because it wasn't.

When my tablemates were tucking into their dessert of chocolate mousse or cheesecake (they had a choice, and both looked tantalizing), God had mercy and I finally broke through the final layer of plastic. Naturally, the aluminum foil made unpleasant crunchy sounds as I tried to fold it neatly and slide it under my plate. After having repeatedly said "No thank you" to the fresh, warm rolls in the breadbasket that circled around the table dizzyingly, I finally got to crack open my own roll (which needed no outside cutting implements) on my newly revealed dinner plate.

Everyone at the table eyed my plastic plate to see the mystery contents. If only it had been a beautifully presented small feast, it might have provided a tiny bit of compensation, but it was only a bland-looking and shockingly small portion of salad, chicken, rice with peas, and roasted summer squash. A Jew's idea of portion control is plunking a second helping on your plate before you are halfway done with your first helping. *Could this really be kosher?* I wondered. I was reminded of an old joke about a Jew complaining about a bad meal he was served in a restaurant. After elaborating on the cuisine's failings, he added, "And such small portions, too!"

Needing to make the best of this fiasco, I joked to my new friends at the table, "Well, after working my biceps and triceps like this, I won't have to lift weights for the next two weeks!" Fortunately, we were all distracted by the excitement of hearing the evening's keynote speaker, Dave Barry. Jeff and I had been ardent fans for years, often reading his work aloud to one another and laughing hysterically. However, this was before we had kids and still had time for such antics as hysterical laughter. I had written to Mr. Barry, asking him if he would gambol through the manuscript of my first book, *Carpool Tunnel Syndrome*, for a possible endorsement. He sent back a gracious and funny refusal, saying he could no longer be known as "the mad warbler" by agreeing to help promote so many books. I understood, but naturally was disappointed.

I couldn't help but notice that in this large crowd, only two people were wearing any sort of hat. Both were women and I was one of them. I wore an elegant brimless hat in a classic Israeli style in a muted green-gray fabric embroidered with tiny, silver beads all around. The other woman wore an enormous duck hat the size of a chimney. Logically, our hats did not belong to the same species of headwear. Irrationally, though, I feared that the ridiculousness of her hat might somehow taint my head covering worn as a sign of Jewish observance.

Her attempt to broadcast her own sense of humor was not lost on Dave Barry, who interrupted his introductory remarks to ask her where she got her hat so that he could get one, too. I held my breath for a moment: would she feel insulted? But Barry was brilliant, his tone deftly blending kindness with a touch of disbelief. The duck hat wearer beamed with delight—with his clever attention, Barry had made her feel honored. That night, my respect for Dave Barry grew, not only because of his fantastically funny yet substantive presentation, but because he knew how to seize an irresistible opportunity for humor that both "used" an audience member while also protecting her dignity. She beamed with delight that he had honored and noticed her.

In the end, I couldn't help it if my tablemates thought keeping kosher was nuts, but at least my hats did me proud. A writer whom I had long admired complimented me on a mauve beret, which led to her endorsing my next book. Standing out through the way I dress, the way I eat, or the way I speak and behave, reminded me that wherever I went, I was a volunteer ambassador for Jewish practice and values, prepared not only to wear different hats but also to face down awkward situations along the way.

Ruff Love with My Third Book

*Outside of a dog, a book is a man's best friend.
Inside of a dog it's too dark to read.*
—Groucho Marx

A few years after publishing *Carpool Tunnel Syndrome*, I got excited about an idea for a book satirizing all manner of diet and exercise fads. Weight control (or lack thereof) had been a lifelong obsession, and I had enormous fun trying military-style workouts and hot yoga (a near-death experience that I do not recommend), listening to the Talmudic hair-splitting discussions in Weight Watchers groups about how to track eating one egg versus two, sampling many awful-tasting sugar-free protein bars, and more. I recorded all my activities and observations, including depressing weigh-ins at Weight Watchers, in a diary-entry format book called *Till We Eat Again: Confessions of a Diet Dropout*.

I loved the book, which was not only cathartic to research and write but also helped me lose twelve pounds. However, finding publishers was still tough, and my book ended up in the hands of a crooked operator. A few years later I hired an attorney to ransom back the rights to my work.

In 2006, with my name recognition a bit less remote and with a highly polished third manuscript, I landed my first literary agent. I had not even tried with my first two books, refusing to waste time on an exercise I knew would be futile. Now, after several years of having my work published steadily, mostly in Jewish media outlets but also through syndication and a few major consumer magazines, I hoped I might succeed.

Uwe was young and had only been an agent for a few years, but he had already earned admission into the Association of American Literary Agents. He was still hungry enough to be interested in a mostly unknown writer who could write well, and he loved the stories that filled *The Women's Daily Irony Supplement.* Uwe had a pronounced German accent and a handsome face that was unmistakably Teutonic. I loved the idea that I had a German literary agent. If he could sell my book, I'd consider it a form of third-generation reparations. Publishers told him that I still had insufficient "platform," though they often published writers with far less platform than I had.

"Your humor is great," Uwe said after sending my proposal to several publishers and being turned down. "But today editors want work that's edgier and more daring, especially if the writers don't have a substantial platform."

I aimed for sharp and incisive humor, but its tone and wholesomeness weren't as salable. Publishers also salivated over books shot through with jaw-dropping, shocking, and seamy levels of dysfunction, yet here, too, I fell short, not having been abused, meth-addicted, or kidnapped and taken to Pakistan by an estranged father.

Still, I might have been a better bet than some authors whose misery-soaked manuscripts had turned out to be frauds. In 2003, Doubleday published James Frey's memoir, *A Million Little Pieces*, which Oprah Winfrey chose for her book club, rocketing him to bestselling status his first time at bat. The book title proved exquisitely prescient. Curious skeptics dug into Frey's lurid claims of drug addiction and extended jail time only to find that they had not been mildly but wildly exaggerated. Oprah got mad. She lassoed him back onto the couch in front of her live audience and said, "I feel duped. But more importantly, I feel that you betrayed millions of readers."

Frey confessed. The audience booed. A million little pieces indeed.

Undeterred, in 2008, a White woman named Margaret Seltzer claimed in a memoir she wrote under the name Margaret B. Jones to have grown up as part American Indian, a foster child in South Central Los Angeles, ensnared into gang life. In fact, she went to a private school in an upper-middle-class suburb of Los Angeles. Her book was published by Riverhead Books with no fact-checking and captured fawning reviews. By the time Seltzer's lies were revealed, the book's title, *Love and Consequences*, also proved deliciously ironic.

While we were both disappointed, Uwe and I agreed that I'd have to find another path to publication. "Thank you for believing in me," I told him. "I know you did your best and I appreciate how hard you worked."

"Thank you for taking a chance on a new agent," he said. "You'll get your book out there, and others will come afterward. Keep in touch."

I had self-published my first book seven years earlier, and since that time, this niche had slowly gained respectability and popularity in the industry, though it was still referred to often as "vanity publishing," even when books went through a vetting process. Despite knowing many authors whose experiences with traditional publishers had been awful, I still craved the mark of distinction conferred by getting a deal inked by a traditional book publisher of stature. But the reality was that this wasn't happening, so I reoriented my thinking and expectations. I worked some of the sting out of my system by writing a satirical story called "It's Not Easy Being Boring," which I slid into the manuscript. It featured a conversation between a literary agent and a writer whose life has been too humdrum to sell: "Okay, work with me here," the literary agent asks me in the story. "Maybe crime isn't your game. How about family dysfunction? Everybody has that! Who in your family was alcoholic? Abusive? Were you molested? I'm sure you were. Everybody is. Traumatized by a psychotic uncle who later had a sex-change operation? I know an editor who'd pay big money now for a story about a psychotic uncle who had a sex-change operation."

The agent pushes me to recall shameful memories that I have repressed. When I confess that I hung up on the only obscene phone call I ever received, he replies: "You never miss an opportunity to miss an opportunity, you know that? . . . You could be sitting on an inspirational story of obsessive infatuations, forgiveness, redemption, and triumph. I see movie rights also."

I protest that as a traditional mom, I'm actually a member of an oppressed minority. "You could be onto something there," he says, pacing the room. "But when you write it, can you at least try to develop a rare, yet curable blood disorder?"

I spent months researching other self-publishing options, checking references relentlessly and asking endless questions. Through the Small Publishers Association of North America, I found Beagle Bay, a small company that agreed to publish *The Women's Daily Irony Supplement* under its Creative Minds imprint. It sounds crazy, but I was drawn to them right away because of their name. I loved beagles, especially Ken, our beagle-lab mix and the four-legged member of the family. Hadn't many successful partnerships been based on flimsier grounds? From the first conversation, I hit it off with Jacqueline, copublisher alongside her husband, Robin. Their beagle was named Bertie, after Bertie Wooster in P. J. Wodehouse's hilarious *Bertie and James* series. A shared love of beagles and even of P. J. Wodehouse wasn't enough research, so I emailed several of their clients, who unanimously vouched for their honesty and professionalism. I was all in.

Like my first book, *The Women's Daily Irony Supplement* was a collection of humor essays about marriage, motherhood, holidays, and women's magnificent obsessions, such as dieting, designer purses, fine chocolates, and comparing oneself to other women of whom you are jealous. After the nightmare experience of having published my second book with a small-time crook masquerading as a publisher, during which I had to ransom the rights to my first and second books at great legal expense, working with Jacqueline was an enormous relief and a pleasure. Finally, I was in good hands—something I did not take for granted.

Many months before publication, a quote I had submitted to Starbucks for their "The Way I See It" series was accepted for printing on approximately five million paper coffee cups. I had been invited to submit three quotes, and, in keeping with the canine theme of my book publisher, they chose this one: "Have you noticed that dogs are the new kids? You take a walk with your kid and your dog, but nobody says, 'What a cute kid!' Instead they say, 'What a cute dog! What's his name? Is he a rescue?' Maybe if I put a collar and leash on my kid someone will notice her."

They wanted to print it right away, but I asked (begged really, almost on my hind legs) them to hold off for several months to coincide with the publishing of my new book. What a PR bonanza! They agreed to hold my quote until I gave them the all-clear, and when the cups had landed in the cafés—the ink barely dry—I went to grab a stash of them on my way to a speaking engagement. I was excited to see the cups and to display them next to my three books at my event. I barreled into the café and rifled through the stack of grande-sized cups on the counter, passing over cups with quotes from the famous, such as Steve Martin, to people I never heard of (my category). I made quick work of extracting four cups and nesting them in a low tower.

"Hey! What are you doing taking those cups!" an irate customer asked me, though no Starbucks baristas seemed to care. I explained that I was only taking cups with my own quote on them.

"What do you mean, *your quote?*" he demanded, yanking a cup from my hand to examine it. He read the quote but didn't laugh or even crack a smile. "You mean you're Judy Green?"

"Gruen. Yes, I'm her." I wanted to get out of there fast, having a growing sense of unease about my speaking gig in a gated community. It was a wealthy crowd, not the kind of group I was used to addressing. Maybe I shouldn't have included those jokes about $4,000 handbags. Well, too late now. I still needed to arrive, get oriented, and set up my little table with my books and my precious, sales-guaranteeing coffee cups.

"Hey, Bob!" Mr. Buttinsky said to his pal, "This lady *says* she's Judy Green and this is her quote on the cup!"

Bob marched over to examine the cup alongside his friend, eyeing me suspiciously. I wanted to evaporate like the mist on a caramel macchiato. If this was a tiny taste of the celebrity life, Jennifer Aniston could have it, and the Dolce & Gabbana sunglasses, too. All I wanted was to write my columns and books and get paid the modest sums I earned for them. Was I going to have to show my driver's license before I could get out of this place with my cups?

The men, both paunchy and middle-aged, peppered me with questions: How'd I get a quote on there? Was I famous or sumpthin? They were standing entirely too close, and I took a step back. They struck me as Winchell's Donut types, not Starbucks types. What were they doing there? While they were still shouting questions, I bolted.

It's a good thing I had two friends with me that evening because next to the extremely elderly, hard-of-hearing Hadassah crowds where I had to shout over their yelling for someone to pass the Splenda, this was the toughest crowd I had ever faced. Certain that my much-practiced performance would be worthy of uploading to my website, I had even hired a videographer. But it was trouble from the moment I arrived at the massive double door, which was slightly ajar. No one answered my knock, and eventually I tiptoed into the foyer, hearing an imperious voice shrilly demanding, "*Where's my speaker?*" I assumed this was the closest I'd get to an invitation to enter the mansion.

The hostess did not even offer me a cup of water or show me where the bathroom was. My friend Laura and I looked at each other with alarm. The heavily Botoxed brigade filed in. No one returned my smiling greetings or even made eye contact. Holy smokes, I was in for it. Who *were* these people? My second friend to rescue me from total social immolation that night was Judi, my editor from my days at UCLA. She lived in this same gated community and sat next to Laura, both of them casting encouraging expressions my way. They laughed sincerely in all the right places (I had practiced in front of Laura, and she knew the drill). The rest of the crowd remained icy. Man, if this is what this much money does to you, I thought, I'd never complain about shopping at Target again.

Indeed, my jokes about Hermes accessories sank like lead as the life lesson "Know your audience!" pounded in my head, triggering a new migraine. By the time I loosened them up and they actually risked a laugh line by chuckling, it was over. The hostess, who had not introduced me with any social grace, was consistent, failing to thank me at the end. Nor did she encourage anyone to buy my book, so Laura and I stood in the small side room, my books and Starbucks cups untouched as the women filed out with barely a glance, probably rushing home to see if their laughter had caused any cracks in their foundation.

Judi invited Laura and me back to her house, which was fortuitous because I was too shaky to drive. I burst into tears in her living room. "I am so embarrassed at this community!" Judi said, aghast. She and Laura reassured me that *I* had been good; the problem was with *them*. Rich crowds were a new species to me. In my crowds, jokes about Rodeo Drive accessories and chronic minivan breakdowns could have gone over big.

Back at home, my family misinterpreted my emotional state for elation over my Starbucks cup. "Wow! Mom's famous!" one kid said. Everyone gathered round the dining room table, where I had set out two cups, marveling as if viewing the British crown jewels in the Tower of London. It was funny how this level of awe over a small life observation used to be reserved for real philosophers, such as Moses or Aristotle. But in our era of instant and pithy messages, all you needed to do was jot down a two-sentence idea that could fit on a throwaway coffee cup and suddenly, you became a somebody!

Just as I began to revive emotionally while nestled in the warmth of my family, one of my teenager's friends, who was hanging around the house as usual, looked at the cup with an appraising eye. I had already begun to fantasize about how the quote would propel my book sales into the stratosphere (as long as people didn't cover it up with those infernal paper sleeves) when this scruffy teen said, "That's so cool, Mrs. Gruen. Try not to think about five million people throwing your name and your quote into the trash when they're done with their coffee." This statement triggered a rude *fantasia interruptus.* I had not had the time to even consider or visualize the crushing, soaking, and destruction of my cups, one by one, expiring in millions of garbage cans across the land. But isn't this one of the benefits of having children? They keep our egos in check.

Dogs continued to nip at my heels, so to speak, with this third book. My weakness for beagles had led me to seek out my publisher. My own dog, Ken, had provided the kibble for my winning Starbucks quote. Meanwhile, Jacqueline had entered *The Women's Daily Irony Supplement* in several industry contests, and I was a finalist in the humor category at the Benjamin Franklin Awards. Jacqueline and I sat together at the ceremony, where I dared to hope that I might take the Gold as we applauded the winners in the other categories. When the humor category was announced, Jacqueline and I straightened our spines, smiling eagerly. On a large overhead screen, the audience viewed huge images of the covers of the three finalists. Jacqueline and I looked at one another, instantly deflated. I would not take the Gold.

My book cover displayed a retro black-and-white photo of a woman from the 1950s, wearing big pearl earrings and a crisp, white dress. She was tipping a medicine bottle into her waiting hand, a sly smile playing on her face. I loved the retro look of the book and its suggestion of ironic humor. But the book cover we immediately knew would take the Gold and had us both licked is etched permanently in my mind: a close-up photo of an impossibly adorable brown Labrador puppy. Who cared what was on the inside pages? They could have been blank and that puppy would still have taken first place.

I only took the Bronze at the Benjamin Franklin Awards, but my book earned *Foreword Reviews* magazine's Book of the Year Award in humor and a Silver IPPY from Independent Publisher. I was more than content with these modest accolades.

Responsibilities

In a time of increasing darkness, we must respond with an increasing of light.
—Rabbi Menachem Mendel Schneerson, Lubavitcher Rebbe

Writing about a topic made you an expert or role model in some people's eyes, even if you weren't. For example, one day I opened an email from "Melissa," who wrote: "I am thirteen years old and very overweight. I was going to ask you if you had any tips for me to help me lose weight without having to suffer. I read one of your stories about the pedometer and walking. I want to be able to loose [sic] weight before I go to high school (next year). Please help me, it would make me so happy if I could feel good about myself."

Melissa had read my story, "Walk a Mile in My Pedometer," in *The Women's Daily Irony Supplement*. I poked fun at my ineptitude in trying to program my pedometer without an embarrassing amount of customer support. Shamelessly, I even insisted that the pedometer was faulty for failing to count my steps accurately and therefore shortchanging the amount of calories burned. (I didn't share that some of those steps had led me to the bakery and a calorically disastrous engagement with a large chocolate chip Danish.) My story was written for laughs, but this young girl was vulnerable and had viewed me as an address for support.

I realized this girl needed professional help, but I could not ignore her, so I wrote back, offering basic, safe suggestions about good nutrition and drinking water. I encouraged her to talk to her parents about her concerns and made it clear that I was not a professional counselor or dietician and that she needed her parents' permission for us to write to one another. Melissa told me in her next email that her mother didn't believe I was a "real author," but she did give Melissa permission to communicate with me.

As Melissa's emails became more revealing, they also became more alarming. She was bored and lonely since moving to a new state, hadn't made many friends, quickly sliding into this condition: "At lunch I would just talk and talk and talk or do anything to keep my mind off of food and it became really easy. But the one day when I fainted in class . . . oh my gosh, it was the worst feeling ever." Though her friends were watching her at lunch now, "it seems harder to eat than not eat," she said.

Melissa dropped to only seventy pounds, and wrote, "I'm not happy about it but like I said it was the one thing I could control in my life. Well I thought I would inform you since you are like my advice person and help leader. I had to get it out to somebody. I'm really thankful that you are helping me out with this. It's easier to say what you want when you don't have to say it to your face, ya know?"

I continued to offer Melissa as much optimism and encouragement as possible, hoping she would get the kind of therapy that would set her on a road to emotional stability and a healthy self-image. Situations like this were rare, fortunately, but my emails with Melissa reminded me of the impact that even a single essay could have—even a humor essay. I could only hope that the support I tried to offer Melissa would tide her over until she got sustained psychological help.

Christian readers had also become part of my fan base, finding common cause with my outlook on family and faith. These points of view were now considered "traditional" or even "conservative," but only one generation earlier they were almost universally agreed upon in society as normative and therefore needed no label. My unwavering identification as a Shabbat-observant Jewish woman who supported Israel was one such value that appealed to these readers. Millions of religious Christians could not understand the leftist views of so many prominent Jews. One reader emailed me in exasperation, "Can you please explain why so many Jewish people do not support the State of Israel? Why do they support so many policies that go against the Bible's teachings?"

What could I say? I didn't want to condemn my own people, but I was more exasperated than they were. Really, did so many people trumpeting their opposition to the Christmas creche on public grounds need to be named Goldberg, Weinstein, or Rosen-Chapman? It was so embarrassing to read about Jews—usually secular—complaining about feeling offended even by such innocent social niceties as "Merry Christmas." We are a numerically microscopic minority in this country and in every single country outside of Israel. Is this a surprise that most people aren't going to shout, "Happy Chanukah!"? They won't offer "*Chag Sameach*" before Pesach, Sukkot, or Shavuot, either. We are known as a stiff-necked people—a trait we have needed for survival. But being so thin-skinned was not a good look for us. In fact, it was obnoxious.

When I would get these kinds of questions, I offered a defense that the Jewish impulse for compassion had gotten many of my coreligionists off track. That impulse runs very deep, and in large measure stems from our history of having been enslaved in Egypt thousands of years ago. The Torah instructs us, "You shall not oppress a stranger, for you know the feelings of the stranger, having yourselves been strangers in the land of Egypt (Exodus 23:9)." This sentiment is repeated in Leviticus 19:33-34: "When a stranger resides with you in your land, you shall not wrong him. The stranger who resides with you shall be to you as one of your citizens; love him as yourself, for you were strangers in the land of Egypt . . .."

When engaging my Christian fans, or even other traditionally minded Jews, I began to see that my outspoken stance as a Shabbat-observant Jew helped to counter the overwhelming sense "out there" that nearly all Jews were politically liberal and their religion, secularism. On the flip side, many Jews all along the religious spectrum were suspicious that Christian motivation to support Israel stemmed from a theological self-interest that Jews would finally accept Jesus as the true Messiah. For many centuries, this had often been true among many Christians, but times had changed. I needed to convince my editor at Aish.com, one of the world's most popular Jewish-content websites, to let me write a feature about Christians United for Israel (cufi.org), the largest pro-Israel organization in the US with more than ten million members and a non-missionizing policy. Their tours to Israel, financial support for dozens of Israel-based organizations, and college campus advocacy on Israel's behalf deserved coverage and thanks from the Jewish community. I can just imagine how these sincere philo-Semites felt each time they saw another Goldberg representing an atheist society campaigning to remove a Ten Commandments monument on public grounds.

Overwhelmingly I wanted my stories to shine the light of Jewish values and wisdom into the world. When I first began studying under Orthodox teachers, my rapidly growing storehouse of knowledge quickly began to blow past its slender borders, exciting my intellect and touching my soul. In some cases, it was a revelation that some of these new ideas were not Christian in origin, as I had thought, but Jewish. Most startling and comforting to me was the concept of an eternal soul. Judaism's emphasis on individual responsibilities over individual rights couldn't have been less trendy, but I believed it was a much healthier approach than our culture's growing and lopsided emphasis on self-fulfillment, emotional expression, and self-compassion. Of course these things are vital. Ironically, though, the more our society encouraged us to focus on our personal happiness and honor our own emotions, the less happy and the more anxious we became.

Judaism's spiritual foundations had added so much to my life yet were invisible to most of the world. I saw that the moral relativism championed by "experts" in Western society was convincing people that there were no hard and fast "rules," only preferences and feelings.

This was so clearly dangerous to society that it drove me closer to my own faith's teachings. Judaism emphasized obligations above personal rights and an emphasis on giving more than receiving. Sure, we had lots of mitzvoth to do and laws to follow, but within healthy frameworks true freedom lies. Our moral and ethical boundaries also protect the most precious relationships in our lives, including our marriages.

In my writing, I looked for opportunities to introduce Jewish teachings and practices that were unknown or misunderstood. One such value I returned to again and again was the concept of *tzniut*. It is usually translated awkwardly as "modesty" but really means a de-emphasis on the physical self in favor of a greater focus on the inner person. It's a lofty and ideal concept, but it crashes into the reality that most women want to be seen as beautiful, understanding that their beauty is a bankable asset, personally and professionally. Like it or not, women are judged on their looks far more than are men.

I was no different. When I was a young, single woman in my early twenties, I constantly measured myself against my competition. I'd look around the room at a party and think, "I'm prettier than she is, but she's got way better legs than I do," among other useless and self-defeating thoughts. Still, the subconscious Orthodox Jewish woman in me must have been clawing to get out because even in those days, I felt that some women were not enhancing their beauty but cheapening themselves by revealing extensive personal assets, or at least strongly suggesting them given that their clothing appeared to have been spray-painted on.

Judaism is real. It acknowledges the power of a woman's beauty. But *tzniut* tempers this by teaching that a woman's inner beauty and personal dignity must be paramount. This is a timeless lesson, but in recent years, with soaring rates of anxiety and depression among adolescent girls and young women tyrannized by endless exposure to digitally altered images of other females in fantasy versions of themselves on social media, true female empowerment requires embracing the concept of *tzniut*. It is a measure of protection for women from secular society's merciless competition to see who can look the youngest, the prettiest, the most alluring. In this way, adopting *tzniut* helps build self-esteem.

A sense of internal value and beauty often springs from a belief in God, who created each of us as a precious individual, and a secure upbringing in a loving home. But millennials and Gen Z have been peeling away from religion in unprecedented numbers. Human nature abhors a vacuum, so in the absence of meaningful spirituality, it's not surprising that people seek fulfillment in the world of physicality, whose limits soon become painfully clear.

In an essay for Aish.com, I described *tzniut* as a gift for both women and men:

> It is a gift for women because it frees us from the stress of feeling we need to compete with other women about how attractive we can be. It liberates us—as women had claimed to want to be liberated—from being viewed primarily as objects and encourages us to be viewed as whole people whose minds and ideas are even more important than our physical attributes.
>
> It is also a gift for men who are very visually driven, and who are now in the no-win situation of working with women who simultaneously demand respect for their professionalism but who dress so provocatively that it is almost a form of sexual harassment. Women can dress attractively and elegantly without compromising their dignity. Isn't that what so much of feminism was supposed to be about?

I was heartened by several reader comments, especially by Jewish women who struggled with *tzniut*—as many women do—and found new understanding and inspiration for it. After all, I had written elsewhere, at a certain point, dignity requires fabric.

Standing Room Only

There are only two types of speakers in the world: the nervous and the liars.
—Mark Twain

There had to be a mistake. I was sure of it. No one in their right mind would have arranged such a lopsided line-up of speakers, all competing against one another for an audience during the same time slot. It was so ludicrous that I laughed out loud when I saw the schedule of authors for Jewish Book Week at American Jewish University, where I would soon discuss *The Women's Daily Irony Supplement*.

Still shaking my head in disbelief, I picked up the phone to call the organizers and alert them to the error. My three competitors were all bestselling writers and celebrities whose books had sold millions: Judith Viorst, who wrote for adults and children, including the hugely successful *Alexander and the Terrible, Horrible, No Good, Very Bad Day*; Rabbi Shmuley Boteach, whose first book, *Kosher Sex*, prompted the *Washington Post* to dub him "Dr. Ruth with a yarmulke;" and at the top of the heap, Spartacus—aka Kirk Douglas. Born Issur Danielovitch Demsky, the Hollywood legend had just published a memoir, *Let's Face It: 90 Years of Living, Loving, and Learning*. And then there was . . . me, author of three humor books that—cumulatively—had sold in the low thousands.

I wasn't exactly a nobody, but far from a *somebody* in terms of renown. My features and essays were published regularly in Jewish and secular media outlets. I had finally broken into writing for major women's magazines including *Ladies Home Journal* and *Woman's Day*. I wrote a monthly column for the Religion News Service syndication, a true source of pride. Having been educated in the secular world, a culture I had embraced until my midtwenties, I now felt uniquely positioned—and motivated—to convey nourishing, traditional Jewish values to a wide audience. Still, facing off against these heavyweights, I felt like a bruised piece of fruit left on the "Last Chance!" rack at the supermarket. So this schedule had to be a mistake.

Right?

"It's not an error," the woman at AJU told me with bureaucratic coolness. "That is your time slot."

"But . . . but . . . *Kirk Douglas?* Viorst and Boteach? Who will come to hear me speak? I might not even come to hear me speak!"

"The schedule is already printed, and the ads are running in the local press," she said with finality. I hung up the phone, gobsmacked. So I guess I'd be speaking to an empty room.

Each November, Jewish Book Week showcases Jewish authors and their new books at festive events nationwide. AJU's event ran for a whole week, but Sunday would draw the biggest crowds, so they stuffed each time slot with several authors to accommodate the literary-minded motherlode. My new book was a collection of humor essays in categories including "A Woman's Home Is Her Hassle," "Reading This Warning Label May Kill You (and Other Observations)," and "Just Wait Till You Have Stretch Marks of Your Own," among others.

I had "auditioned" for this opportunity months earlier in New York, where I had traveled at my own expense to make my pitch to a room filled with Jewish book week organizers from throughout North America. Hosted by the Jewish Book Council, it was like speed dating for authors and event organizers. Every author or their publisher had paid handsomely to participate, and each of us had 120 seconds to make the sale. Anyone still jawing when the two minutes were up heard a bell ring as a program official off to the side said, "Your time is up." The sound of those words had an awful finality to them.

It's much tougher to speak meaningfully and memorably in two minutes than if you have ten minutes. Every word must add value. I knew I was a good speaker. Despite my speaking debacle a few months earlier among the Botox Brigade in that gated community, I had hit a home run as a keynote speaker at a conference (at AJU, in fact) attended by more than three hundred women and had done well at a smattering of much smaller (and unpaid) events.

But there had also been one more fiasco, years earlier in St. Louis. At that Jewish book week event, based on a coin toss that I lost, I was forced to speak immediately after a lean and glamorous New York television broadcaster who showed up with a personal handler. My mouth went dry as I watched as she purred to the audience, ambling among them in her Prada pumps like a goddess sprinkling fairy-dust blessings of confidence, elegance, and wealth. She was everything that I was not, and I sat there with my typed speech, hands trembling, heart knocking, and head throbbing, awaiting the apocalypse. It was a train wreck that left me physically ill for two days afterward. On a sunnier note, I learned two new hard-won lessons: *never* read from a script and never agree to a coin toss to determine whether I spoke before or after a glitzy, high-profile media star whose shoes cost more than my oven.

Yet somehow, despite how much was on the line, my brain froze each time I began to prepare for the Jewish Book Council. My book didn't have much actual Jewish content, but it did have a lot of Jewish humor. One of my favorite stories recounted the time I had revived a half-dozen sick relatives who all went viral with a nasty cold while staying in my house. They all languished pathetically until they were roused by the aroma of hot Lo Mein and Kung Pao Chicken that I had delivered for dinner. One by one, they began shuffling toward the table, inhaling the bouquet of the real Jewish penicillin.

That trip to New York to make my two-minute sales pitch seemed ill-fated from the start. I was seized with a crippling headache the night before my flight; rising at 4:30 a.m. to get to the airport was torture. I desperately needed a massage or chiropractic treatment, neither of which would be available for a day or more. At the airport, I stopped to stare at a display rack in front of a bookstore—every slot was filled with a copy of Sara Gruen's *Water for Elephants*, which only discharged the nuclear warheads in my blinding headache. I stared at the correct last name but the wrong first name and the wrong book title. Sara Gruen had become an overnight literary star with her first book, and I nearly burst with unholy jealousy. Instead of writing about dogs, elephants, or a Bildungsroman shot through with bleakness and abuse, I was writing like Erma Bombeck—if she had had two sets of dishes and drove ten carpools a week. I'd never become airport bookshop bait.

My outfit also proved to be a wardrobe malfunction. This new oatmeal-colored skirt was too long to be flattering on my short figure; I might as well have been dressed for the reboot of *Little House on the Prairie*. And it couldn't have been a worse choice to navigate the stinky, sticky stairwells of the New York subway system either. After traipsing from Brooklyn to Manhattan in my linen prairie outfit, I looked like an accordion by the time I arrived at the hall.

And so, for the first time in my life, when I was called to the podium to make my two-minute pitch, I was inexcusably ill-prepared. I smiled at the audience and waved my book cover in front of them, as if the sight of it might hypnotize them and convince them to fly me to Seattle or Toronto or Chicago to entertain their audiences. Ultimately, that was my angle: the healing and restorative power of humor, something Jews understood very well. Why else were we so wildly overrepresented in the fields of comedy and humor?

At the end of the evening, I simply felt relief that it was over. I'd have plenty of time for self-flagellation on the long flight home. Walking out of the hall, I struck up a conversation with "Irene," a first-time author whose historical novel about the daughter of a famous religious sage had become a darling among new Jewish releases. While this was the first in a planned series, Irene had already sold the next two to a big New York publisher. I had read the book, impressed by the amount of research she had done and her skillful writing style. However, I didn't like the way that she had given her protagonist—who lived in the Middle Ages—a decidedly twenty-first-century outlook, particularly on matters of sexuality. This was a savvy strategy from a marketing standpoint, but I felt it bordered on the sacrilegious.

Irene was warm, gracious, and had worked hard to achieve her success. We stood on the dark street together for quite a while, swapping stories about our writing and publishing experiences, until she hailed a taxi (paid for by her New York publisher) to take her to a nice hotel (paid for by her New York publisher). In my dumb, impractical outfit, I hoofed it back to the smelly, sticky subway steps and onto the train that would rattle me back to Brooklyn, where I was bunking down in a creaky old apartment with a friend.

As my engagement at AJU drew near, I consulted with a public speaking expert who helped clients deliver their messages to key audiences with power and panache. She reinforced the most important lesson I ever would learn about public speaking: know my subject, stories, and ideas well enough that I could improvise as needed. It was so obvious once she said it and a relief as well. Of course I knew my stories! Why had I even felt captive to a script in the first place?

"Just have an index card or two with a few keywords and phrases written down as prompts if you need them," Sarah counseled. "That's all you need." Her priceless advice helped me retool my whole approach to public speaking. No more worrying over giving a memorized speech and blanking out in the middle of a sentence. My style and delivery improved immediately—a bonus for both me and my audiences.

I corralled my son Noah to come with me to the Sunday event.

(Oddly, everyone else in my family suddenly had other plans...) At least I could deliver my talk to *him* if no one else showed up! My shabby treatment by the program organizers continued that day. Not only had they tossed me into a teeny room stuffed with a few oversized chairs, but they hadn't even bothered to tape up a sign indicating where I would be speaking or how to follow the maze of hallways to arrive at this little mystery closet. Meanwhile, Spartacus held court in the big theater on campus; Viorst and Rabbi Boteach were in halls that could hold a few hundred.

My biggest victory was that I had made peace with the situation. Even if no one showed up, I decided to be happy that I had prepared a terrific talk, with only two small index cards with a few prompting phrases and words. I was comforted that my son Noah was with me, and he was a good listener. So when one person who was unrelated to me opened the door, I nearly threw myself at him in gratitude. Then another person came. And another. And another! Five people in all—standing room only! I had been the first choice of these intrepid souls from a menu of A-listers and me, considerably further down on the celebrity food chain. I told my stories from the heart and didn't need any script for that. It was the smallest audience I ever had, but the one I appreciated the most.

Boundaries

Writers are always selling somebody out.
—Joan Didion

In the early 2000s, the blogosphere floodgates opened, and "mommy bloggers" delivered more blogs than Orthodox Jews produced kids. Through this medium, moms found creative self-expression about their lives and a way to build a sense of community. The entrepreneurial-minded among them built substantial readerships that in turn allowed them to sell advertising space and post other sponsored content. Some found modest celebrity, clinching gigs as paid sponsors of kiddie products and services. I had published my own blog for many years but wasn't entrepreneurial enough to know how to really grow the audience. Instead, I piggybacked on the popular site MommaSaid.net, the brainchild of writer Jen Singer, and posted my work on her much-better known website.

Most of the independent mom blogs I came across were sweet, sometimes funny, often tender. But a few bloggers were willing to write almost anything for public consumption to satisfy their need to express themselves emotionally. One writer with thousands of Facebook followers posted: "I am not speaking to my daughter right now. She is acting like a little s— so we are taking a break from one another."

I was appalled at this writer's selfishness. Sure, writers are hardwired to shop for material through their own lives and experiences, as well as the lives and personalities of others around them. I did, too. It's one thing to "borrow" people and their experiences for material in your work in ways that do not exploit them. It's another entirely to "borrow" in ways that do. Sometimes it's a gray area, but to me, this clearly crossed the line. I read the entire post only to discover that it was, at heart, a sweet story about the kinship between her daughter and son, who had been in league against their mommy for some small reason or another. This made her exploitation of the situation more contemptible, in my view. She also posted photos of her children online, and they could not have been more than six and eight years old.

More than five hundred people "liked" her post. But I was riled up and offered a dissent, suggesting that her profane and angry column could easily hurt her child's feelings, if not now, then later. Young children are sensitive and often have an inner fragility they try to cover up. Content can live forever online. How many millions of adults are keeping thousands of therapists in business still unpacking the emotional wounds from callous or hurtful words said by parents twenty, thirty, or even forty years earlier? You didn't have to be a mother to realize this, but if you were a mother, how could you not see? I wasn't surprised when the writer—whose columns were often saturated with profanities—dismissed my comment as ridiculous, even undeserving of having been said. This was rich! She claimed the right to be completely uninhibited, but I should just shut up instead of voicing any objection. Her children were secure in her love, she retorted, "but thanks for worrying."

In an essay about this topic for the *Chicago Tribune* titled, "Should Bloggers Rant Online About Their Kids?" I argued:

> Love is more than a word; it's a pattern of speech and actions where crude invective has no place, particularly where young children are involved. Maybe her children are so used to their mother's potty-mouthed patois that bleep-worthy words

don't even register. If so, what a shame that they have already become so desensitized to the power of language. There are words that elevate and there are words that degrade. In today's coarsened culture . . . it is infinitely harder to convey the damage done by careless and caustic language.

Judaism teaches the value of discretion, of scrupulously trying to select my words with care. It helped me feel how much of a privilege I enjoyed in being published on a regular basis. It was a responsibility I took seriously and tried to honor by doing good with my work. The concept of *lashon hara* (bad or evil speech) is a huge deal in Judaism. Speaking negatively about others—and even about ourselves—is forbidden unless there is a compelling, valid reason for doing so. For example, if you are considering going into business with someone or marrying them (the ultimate business!), then sharing relevant, negative information is justified. But there's a reason we have the expression "to die of embarrassment." Words are so easily weaponized, sometimes to devastating effect.

I was fired up when I wrote that essay for the *Chicago Tribune*. Didn't kids have a hard enough time growing up feeling secure and confident without having parents who were Bloggers Without Borders? Even the most resilient children have sensitive souls, often concealing hurts that simmer beneath the surface for years, afraid to reveal them for fear of parental disapproval. Those hidden hurts can corrode relationships or contribute to poor self-esteem.

I also quoted Elizabeth Shatzkin, a marriage and family therapist, who observed, "For every one of these degrading, destructive moments in a child's life, they need ten solid building moments to overcome the weight of it. Children learn to hold feelings and confusion inside to avoid further hurt. This is highly destructive to their self-worth, and I see the results in clients of all ages."

In our confessional society, too many people had elevated the value of "being real," "staying sane," and "stating my truth" over classic values such as restraint and consideration for the privacy of others. Some parent bloggers went so far as to write about evenings where they drank to excess, or fantasies in which they hurt their children. (Just a thought: could the first activity have led to the other?) Not just bloggers but journalists published articles in major media outlets or in books about their children's own emerging sexuality or mental health issues, exposing their children's intimate, emotional lives in ways that could not be retracted. But I bet they made sure their kids wore helmets when they went biking! Maybe they bought organic apples, too. Physical dangers they understood. Psychological and emotional dangers from their unfiltered posts, not so much.

I hadn't always appreciated the boundaries. Early on, I showed one column that I knew might be too revealing to a trusted friend. She bluntly said, "You can't write about your child's troubles in school like that. It's hurtful." It hadn't struck me that way, but I had a niggling concern that it might be "off," which was why I showed it to my friend. There were ways around the problem with my column, such as universalizing the issue, but stories never work as well when they are made more generic. I tabled the story, spooked that I had allowed myself to have gotten so caught up in *my* writing and *my* self-expression that I had become desensitized to the story's potential impact on my child.

It's tempting to let it all hang out. I get that. Truthfully, there have been times I wished I could have shared my life more openly with readers. Some events were just so funny that I imagined the hilarity my stories could induce. Other situations were very serious, and I believed the lessons I had learned from them could be helpful to others. But at what cost? Unless a writer is a hermit, when they write about their life, they're never writing about themselves alone. Others get roped into the storyline, knowingly or not. While I've had to leave precious material on the proverbial cutting room floor, I knew I'd rather stay married and have my kids continue to talk to me than add some laughs or drama at my loved ones' expense. I hoped that even without my discovery and adherence to Jewish teachings I would have had this sense of discretion on my own, but given my natural appetite for ambition, how could I really have been certain?

Over the years my kids were sometimes taken by surprise when community members or friends would discuss our family news with them. They'd come home and ask, "Mom, did you just do a column about my taking driving lessons?" Or, "Mom, did you just write about helping me with my school science project?" These were tame topics where I had full certainty that nobody would mind. But sometimes I was warned off a topic: "Mom, do NOT write about this!" commanded my daughter the minute she realized that the cake recipe she was following had called for one cup of *brewed* coffee, and not one cup of coffee crystals. Please try to appreciate my level of self-restraint in holding that one back for so many years.

As the kids got older, I'd ask permission before I wrote about anything that involved them directly, or situations where they could easily be identified. Overall, my family members have been great sports about my scribbling about us, because what better material is out there more colorful, more outrageous, more heart-tugging than relatives? At one writers' conference I became friendly with another humorist whose first book, also family-focused, had become a bestseller. It was a terrific book, and I envied his commercial triumph. He also wrote a popular column for a Midwest newspaper that leaned heavily on family for column fodder. When we met for lunch one day in LA, he told me he was getting divorced. I felt terrible for him: what would he write about now, I wondered?

Follow the Blessing

Talent is God-given. Be humble. Fame is man-given. Be grateful. Conceit is self-given. Be careful.
—John Wooden

Jewish sages teach us to "flee from honor," but today everyone is a self-promoter. If you have a business or product, you need to let the world know about it, hourly if possible. Glamour shots for your website, even if you're a dog groomer, may be recommended. The last time anyone could simply hang the proverbial shingle announcing their new stationery store or insurance brokerage and wait for the public to storm the battlements, gas was cheap and climate change meant the November wind was blowing and it was time to button your jacket.

This teaching to flee from honor is obviously wise: self-regard can quickly become an addiction, leading to dangerous cravings for flattery, fame, and tribute. On the other hand, authors need to sell their books. "Books don't have legs," one publicist told me. "You've got to keep working it over and over again for at least one year after publication. Keep promoting, keep writing, and keep making sure your byline includes the 'author of' attribution at the bottom. Talk it up wherever you go, post on social media, pass out bookmarks. Stay positive." In other words, don't flee from honor; stalk it at every opportunity!

I was pumped for the game after my first few books. I believed in my work, in the therapeutic power of humor, in the value of intelligent, family-friendly writing that could entertain and inspire.

I burned through a lot of cash on publicists and burned through a lot of psychic energy from my efforts following their directives. Yet I began to feel like the proverbial hamster on the wheel. The media world was evolving at breakneck speed and so were the "rules" about how to "grow your brand" as a writer. I was advised to blog three times a week (supposedly a magic number), offer giveaways on my home page to capture email addresses, and become a topic expert for reporters, replying to their queries through member-only PR sites.

Given my strong beliefs about what our culture was doing to our kids, I promoted myself to parenting expert, frequently offering bite-sized commentary to reporters. My contributions were picked up on occasion, but my overall batting average was low, the return on investment hardly seeming worth my time. I contacted book reviewers, social media influencers, and other potentially friendly media outlets about my books—and about me! As the meme goes, "But enough about me; what do *you* think of me?"

I threw myself into it, chasing book reviews, interviews, and buzz. Honor didn't exactly flee from me, but it hardly threw its arms open wide, reaching toward me with a beguiling smile and asking, "Darling, where have you been all my life?" I did my job cheerfully for a long time. Then I did it dutifully. Then, though I still believed my work was valuable, promotion began to feel like a heavy lift. At this stage in the media world, effective promotion involved engaging with your audience to foster a sense of connection and trust. But connecting takes time, and I was also juggling paid writing and editing work and family responsibilities. I enjoyed the engagement, but it sure would be easier to continue building credibility and awareness through being published regularly where my readers could be found.

Once I ran into a casual acquaintance who had—almost on a lark—written a book about marriage and had signed with a respected traditional publisher. When I asked her how she was promoting her book, she shrugged. "I wrote it and I believe it's good, but I can't get into all the work of publicity," she said. This shocked me and I imagined her publisher wasn't too thrilled about it, either. It was a wasted opportunity because her book contained valuable messages that could touch people's lives. Part of me admired her sangfroid, which contrasted dramatically with my own angst and nervous energy in trying to build my books' fortunes.

After so many years of hard, relentless work, my following still was relatively small, so I reminded myself of another Jewish teaching: *I have everything in my life that I need right now to fulfill my mission. What is meant for someone else is not meant for me.* I worked to cement this idea into my head; it felt true and wise and necessary for me to grasp. Besides, what number of books sold or number of fans would have satisfied me? I didn't even know! My definition of success had been evolving, and I understood that it could not be quantified only by hard numbers of books sold, readers reached, and social media affirmations. People told me that my writing mattered to them, either in person, through emails, social media, in letters to the editor or in online comments about my stories.

In a culture where traditional values about marriage, family, education, patriotism, and religion were mercilessly and endlessly mocked by cultural arbiters in journalism, publishing, and the entertainment industries, my articles helped other like-minded individuals feel more supported and less alone. A few college-aged women emailed me to say they related to my work and in particular, my fifth book, a memoir called *The Skeptic and the Rabbi: Falling in Love with Faith*. "I feel like you are writing my story," one twenty-two-year-old college senior wrote. "I also have a boyfriend who is becoming Orthodox, and I'm getting into it but also not sure if I'll change my mind later. You've given me a lot to think about. I'll keep you posted!" Notes like this made my work so worthwhile. You couldn't put a dollar value on playing a role in helping someone clarify their goals.

Still, I couldn't slay the dragon of career ambition, that sense that the success I felt I deserved—ill-defined and perhaps shallow as it was—would continue to elude me. In fact, certain goals I had nourished for years were receding out of reach. Traditional print newspapers were folding by the hundreds each year, so I stopped pitching newspaper syndicates. Pay scales for online writing were even more pathetic than they were in most print journalism outlets, and hundreds of journalists were nimbly transitioning into "content creation" or other types of writing for corporations and institutions that would pay enough for them to survive.

When I'd become grumpy about all this, Jeff did his best to encourage me. "Your work will never be measured by dollars and cents or even by the number of books you sell," he'd say, reiterating the lesson I knew but still struggled to accept. "Your work inspires people, and in some cases, you actually change lives. I just run a small sign company. My work is a means to an end—nothing more."

I'd immediately argue with him. "Your work is much more than that. You have succeeded through your intelligence, hard work, industry knowledge, honesty, integrity, and ability to communicate well. Your services and consulting help other people run their own businesses and organizations. And your stellar reputation is a *kiddush Hashem* (a credit to God's name, so to speak) because everyone knows you are an Orthodox Jew. These are not small things. They're huge." Every once in a while, we'd reprise this same friendly "argument," each of us needing reassurance about the larger impact and meaning of our work.

After one such discussion, before my doldrums had fully lifted, I decided to consult with a woman named Rachel. Like me, Rachel had become Orthodox in early adulthood but unlike me, had raised her family in Israel, where she studied Judaism from a mystical angle. Personally, I am mystically challenged and hadn't planned on attending Rachel's classes when she visited Los Angeles during a speaking tour. A friend raved about her, though, and I figured, why not? Rachel's topic for the class I attended was the Jewish perspective on male-female polarities and the creative forces and energy associated with women.

Rachel explained that men often contribute the raw material of life—the potential—while women are the ones who actualize that material, turning it into something tangible. This is an obvious truth in procreation, but even when women also contribute the raw material (such as money earned to support their families), they are also the ones who most often actualize it: shopping for groceries, doing most of the cooking, and making most home-based purchasing decisions, from furnishings and décor to children's clothing and selecting extracurricular activities for the children. Through their material and spiritual priorities, women set the tone of a home and family life. This has an enormous impact on each family member, and that impact is carried through future generations.

I was drawn to Rachel's understated tone and deep wisdom. While some of her ideas and practices felt overly traditional or mystical for my taste, her fundamental idea about male-female polarities and women's creative potential rang true. After class I made an appointment to speak with her the next day.

When I arrived for our meeting, she greeted me with a smile that felt like a hug. We sat down in the comfortable living room of the private home where she was staying during her trip. I knew full well that Rachel was undoubtedly counseling other women seeking advice on far more urgent problems than mine, problems relating to their marriages, kids, financial pressures, or spiritual crises. I felt a flush of embarrassment at my "first world" kvetch: *You see, Rachel, I've been working so hard to become a successful writer, but I'm not successful enough! I want to be successful in the material sense of the word and I can't seem to tame the beast of my ambition, which is suffocating my deeper wisdom. Can you help?*

But there I was, and I began to talk. As I talked, I unexpectedly began to cry. Rachel leaned slightly closer to me, her eyes kind and empathetic.

"I really love the writing I do for Jewish media outlets," I told her. "People in the community often stop me on the street or in shul or in the market to comment about something I wrote, and when they smile and tell me how much they enjoyed an article, I feel great. But when I see so many trashy or stupid books become big sellers or books that were written to knock Jewish tradition or malign Israel, I become extremely upset, even angry. It's so wrong and unfair. My books aren't of earth-shaking importance, but they are well-crafted and lift people's spirits. After so many years of trying, I still have to scrape for every review and endorsement."

Oh man, I sounded like such a whiner! What would she think of me? Hearing my own bellyaching, I didn't think much of myself at that moment. But the catharsis was desperately needed, and I felt an oppressive weight of angst lifting. Rachel listened as if my words were the most important ones she had ever heard. I stopped, feeling so self-conscious about my emotional rant, but she recognized that I had more inside and urged me to go on.

I told her of my growing disillusionment with the industry, including the impossibility of meeting marketing "rules" that were constantly changing. I told her of having finally broken through to write for some of the biggest women's magazines that had left me starry-eyed for years only to find their editors ridiculously difficult to work with. It was especially ironic that these women editors demonstrated some of the worst stereotypes about females, just as their editorial angles were strongly feminist: they constantly changed their minds about what they wanted after assignments had been defined and asked for numerous revisions without offering any justification or extra pay. Their high-maintenance reputation was legendary among writers, and after only a few assignments the bloom had definitely faded from the rose. A buck per word sounded like great pay until you were asked for seven revisions.

"I know I am meant to do this work," I continued, "and I know I have something valuable to add to the cultural conversation, but the leftward agenda of nearly all of the US newspapers and consumer magazines makes it much harder to sell stories where I sold them before, even when the Jewish messages are subtle. Maybe I just can't seem to get past the idea that money equals success, which Western culture has ingrained in me. Is it wrong to want to spread Torah ideas and to want to be commercially successful?" I dabbed at another tear and offered a small smile, feeling embarrassed and vulnerable.

Rachel's frequent, subtle nods and caring expression assured me that I had come to the right address for handholding. I observed something else about her, too. Living in a city that might be the nipping, tucking, derma-filling, liposuction capital of the world, where looking older than thirty-five is a misdemeanor, Rachel—without any makeup and most likely in her late forties or possibly early fifties—was beautiful. I had observed a certain radiance and loveliness in many deeply religious Jewish women I had met whose focus in life is primarily other-centered, and specifically, God-centered. They are looking at the Big Picture—how to create a bit of heaven here on earth through actualizing the mitzvah, giving more than taking, and building their eternity. They exude an inner glow born of a spiritual centeredness that is almost palpable. Their faces reflect kindness, faith, and confidence. Like Rachel, they are often lovely and luminous.

When I finished emptying my cup of woes, Rachel lifted a cup of water to her lips. Before she sipped, she closed her eyes and quietly spoke the appropriate blessing: *Blessed are You, God, King of the entire world, who makes everything according to His Word.* She enunciated each Hebrew word with a level of consciousness and care I had rarely, if ever, witnessed before.

Her blessing humbled me. We are meant to recite one hundred blessings each day, a majority of which are covered through the morning, afternoon, and evening prayer sessions. I did not pray with that level of frequency and so far had been a chronic blessing underachiever. You'd think that for the blessings I *did* make, including those before and after eating and drinking, I could have mustered something close to a Rachel-esque level of *kavana*, or intent. But my mind was cluttered, often fighting off competing thoughts about my quotidian life while trying to make space to talk to God: *Do I have enough panko for tonight's schnitzel? When can I get to the store to get the rest of the materials for the school science project? Who should we invite for Shabbat dinner this week? What should my next column be about? I need a haircut; I wonder how soon I can get an appointment?* After Rachel set her glass down, she asked a profound question that no marketing expert would have ever asked me: "Tell me, Judy, where is the blessing coming from now in your work?"

I was stunned. I had appreciated the positive feedback and the affirmations about the meaning of my work, but never considered my "success" as Rachel had framed it. Instead, I kept fixating on the mundane and the materialistic: How many social media shares was I getting? How much does this outlet pay? When would I reach out to introduce myself to the editor at a new target media outlet?

The answer came immediately: "The blessing is coming from my work in Jewish media." As soon as the words left my mouth, both her question and the answer seemed so obvious. I had welcoming editors who provided straightforward assignments and direct, blunt feedback, great freedom about what I wrote about, and an impressive platform for my work.

I had always loved writing profiles and discovering the fascinating stories of people's lives. Ahuva Gray was a Black former preacher who converted to Judaism and moved to Jerusalem. Dr. Edith Eger barely survived the Holocaust and became a prominent psychologist specializing in PTSD. In her nineties, she published the remarkably powerful book, *The Choice*. The rock group Eagles of Death Metal chose to play a concert in Tel Aviv just months after surviving a terrorist attack by Islamic terrorists during a performance at the Bataclan Theater in Paris, owned by a French Jew. The terrorists killed ninety and wounded hundreds more, including some band members. These are just some of the inspiring people I'd had the privilege to learn and write about. Research I did for my stories expanded my knowledge and my world. And it would have been churlish of me to deny that my steady publishing credits were adding to my name recognition in Jewish circles. The Jewish outlets consistently welcomed me, allowing me to create in the way I was meant to create.

I left my meeting with Rachel feeling lighter for my whinging session. Ever so slightly, I felt even more successful. Neither Rachel nor I could solve the growing obstacles to my breaking through to a larger audience. Publishing and journalism were becoming siloed into the political left or right. Most journalists and editors in the legacy media were increasingly arrested by storylines that validated leftist talking points and jeered traditional religious values. Articles began to appear in women's and parenting magazines celebrating parents who supported their nine-year-olds who had decided they were now a boy, not a girl, or vice versa. These were kids who were not old enough to pick their own bedtimes. Magazines for teen girls promoted promiscuity, with no warning about the well-documented psychological harm that frequently resulted from that behavior. While sinking educational outcomes for kids in public schools was a growing problem, no one at the *Washington Post* covered stories about the success of kids who were homeschooled (usually from religiously traditional families) or the success of kids in charter schools, where minority children often thrived outside the chokehold of terrible public schools. Rap singers with long rap sheets were interviewed by reporters who seemed awed by the singer's toughness and who asked no hard questions about the singer's violent past. The bias was incredible and nearly universal.

I could not afford to waste my time and chose to scale back my efforts to write for the secular media, only looking for opportunities to write on health, relationships, and aspects of culture where I could sprinkle in some subtle Jewish wisdom. For the most part, my professional contributions to *tikkun olam* would have to be "locally sourced," writing for Jewish media outlets with a broad and growing audience. It was my responsibility to take action to achieve important goals. I could only hope my work would have some impact.

Responding to the Jewish Misery Memoir Market

Memoir is how we try to make sense of who we are, who we once were, and what values and heritage shaped us... a good memoir is also a work of history, catching a distinctive moment in the life of both a person and a society.
—William Zinsser, Inventing the Truth

Turning the pages of a popular Jewish periodical to the book review section, I looked at the book cover, inhaled deeply and thought, *here we go again.* Shulem Deen's memoir, *All Who Go Do Not Return* chronicled his life as a member of a Hasidic community in New York, his growing feelings of claustrophobia within it, and eventual break from it. In the rigid religious standards of his community, his casting off of his Orthodoxy also meant a painful divorce and losing custody of his five children.

Although the trend had begun in 2008 with *Foreskin's Lament: A Memoir*, by Shalom Auslander, an author who referred to his upbringing in the Orthodox community of Monsey, New York, as having been "raised like veal," 2015 turned out to be a banner year for anti-Orthodox memoirs, most taking aim at Hasidic communities. Shulem Deen's story covered much of the same ground as the memoirs *Uncovered* by Leah Lax and *Exodus* by Deborah Feldman. *Exodus* had been a follow-up to Feldman's 2012 bestseller, *Unorthodox: The Scandalous Rejection of my Hasidic Roots,* destined to become a Netflix miniseries. Simon & Schuster published Feldman's first memoir despite the first-time author's lack of platform or previous publishing credits. With a mother who abandoned her, a father with mental health issues, and an oppressive religious community, Feldman checked all the dysfunction boxes that would make her book marketable. *Unorthodox* was widely praised as "harrowing yet triumphant," and "compulsively readable." The *Huffington Post* wrote, "No doubt girls all over Brooklyn are buying this book, hiding it under their mattresses, reading it after lights out—and contemplating, perhaps for the first time, their own escape." No doubt! The Jewish Book Council, the main clearinghouse for new books of Jewish interest, reviewed nearly every one of these memoirs, even though of necessity they can only review a small fraction from among the hundreds of new Jewish book titles each year.

Some novelists also got into the act. Eve Harris's *The Marrying of Chanie Kaufman,* published in 2013, was an unforgivably awful book filled with anti-Orthodox vitriol. Nearly every character harbors secret antipathy, resentment, despair, and unmet desires due to their living according to Torah values and laws. The author's bigotry is unending: the women wear "mousy wigs," Jewish mothers have to shift their "ample backsides" to make room for a third person to sit near them; the wedding hall is filled with "the stink of body odour and stale breath." The rabbi's beard is "greasy;" kitchen floors in these homes are of "sticky linoleum;" and, as if all this were not damning enough, women wear polyester nightgowns to bed. Now, Jews have been accused of many a vile crime, but having to carry the load of wearing cheap polyester to bed is a new low. *The Marrying of Chanie Kaufman* was long-listed for the Man Booker Prize in 2013.

From this bounty of anti-Orthodox memoirs, I decided to read Shulem Deen's due to its excellent reviews by people I trusted. His was a heartbreaking story about his loss of faith and eventually his inability to continue living a double life. While no longer believing in God or in the values of his Hasidic community, he understood its boundaries and its need to protect itself through insularity. He wrote of his pain with skill, sensitivity, restraint, and humor.

My heart goes out to anyone stuck in a life that feels inauthentic and constricting. Our mission in life is to discover who we are meant to be and how best to fulfill our potential. This can take years of soul searching, as well as trial and error. Many memoirs—including these just mentioned—were born of pain. Everyone who wants to write a memoir has the right to do so, but I was also pained, as well as frustrated and even angry that the only memoirs capturing widespread attention with the adjective "Orthodox" attached to them were anti-Orthodox. These writers reflected Judaism from its strictest, narrowest borders. Their emergence reflected true and troubling problems in those communities, but their appearance in the book market within a few years of one another presented a skewed, prejudiced, and condescending vision of Torah life as outdated, oppressive, and sexist. If it was that bad for everyone, women's wigs would have been flying off en masse in Williamsburg, New York, and there would suddenly be a glut of unsellable black frock coats throughout Brooklyn.

The Orthodox world—a surprisingly broad term that can't begin to convey the robust number of subcategories within it—has dysfunction. What community doesn't? And yes, there are bad actors wearing yarmulkes and keeping kosher who might also be hypocrites, cheats, petty tyrants, or other sinful things that create a *chillul Hashem*—a desecration of God's name. Some people may be emotionally troubled in ways that skew their thinking and behavior, creating a cascading effect of trouble. The damage inflicted by these individuals naturally pushes people away, especially those who were looking for an escape route in the first place. But this is a story as old as time. Even in the days of ancient Israel when God's open miracles were still common, we had our bad actors, too.

Free choice guarantees that we will always have such people—until the Messianic era. If everyone did exactly as we should only because we'd instantly be rewarded or punished for our actions, we wouldn't be humans with agency. We'd be robots. This is what makes the selflessness, dignity, moral achievements, and goodness of most religious Jews so inspiring. Most strive each day to live with wholesomeness, soulfulness, integrity, and goodness. Self-reflection is built into our daily lives. The secular world never sees the endless efforts of religious Jews to study, to perform mitzvoth and acts of kindness, to rise as a community to pray for and assist others in need, and to admit our failings and seek forgiveness, knowing that God is on our team, cheering us on in our growth.

By the time these Orthodox-shaming memoirs were published there were many thousands of *baalei teshuva* like me—people who had been raised and educated in the secular world but who had chosen a deeper engagement with Judaism's original, unvarnished teachings and practice. The religious life I lived, and that the vast majority of other Orthodox Jews whom I knew personally lived, was far more diverse, accepting, and broadminded than the lives portrayed by these memoirists. Frankly, it was people like us, the baalei teshuva, who deserved a bit of respect. We had made the counter cultural decision to reclaim our spiritual heritage, bringing our enthusiasm as well as secular knowledge and skills to the Orthodox Jewish world. Marrying and having families, we had added tens of thousands of children into the Jewish ranks that were otherwise being decimated through intermarriage, assimilation, and having few or no children.

After World War II, many Jews and non-Jews had predicted the demise of Orthodox Judaism. And yet, another miracle of Jewish revival occurred—another in a series of hundreds throughout history. Thousands of Jews were choosing to keep the Sabbath, keep kosher, and study the 3,300-year-old Torah as a path for living. We were defying the dominant secular culture, and in doing so we were changing the face of the modern Jewish world. Where were our stories?

Back in college as an intern with the Jewish Student Press Service, I had interviewed a few young baalei teshuva. I found their stories fascinating, but it was almost purely an intellectual exercise. Their lives seemed so foreign to me, with so many children and seemingly so cut off from the secular world. I couldn't have imagined that life. I did not know of the variety of Orthodox "flavors," and didn't realize I could still be me as an Orthodox Jew. I didn't understand that this commitment would be transformational and expansive.

Writers who fled their unhappy Orthodox lives weren't the only ones who had felt alienated from their communities and cultures. Religious Jews also felt disenfranchised from a society that increasingly viewed traditional marriage and family structure as oppressive and patriarchal, elevated feelings over self-discipline, and erased boundaries between the personal and the public, the sacred and profane. Baalei teshuva in particular often faced chiding disapproval by family members and rejection by friends for our choices. The mainstream media had zero curiosity about us and totally missed this story of an unexpected religious Jewish renaissance.

I had a choice: I could simply remain incensed about the fanfare granted these dark, dreary, and dysfunctional portraits of Orthodox Jewish life, or I could take a stand. Increasingly, I felt protective of my tribe. Determination soared inside me: I could not and would not let those unhappy memoirists speak for me. Yet writing a memoir had never been a goal, and this would be a hugely challenging project, far more difficult than the lighter books I had produced so far. It would take a few years of effort. And based on the appetites of traditional and even most indie publishers, who would even want to publish it? I feared it would be a book that was needed but not wanted.

Thinking about the publishing world's current appetites brought to mind this observation by the character of Betta Nolan from Elizabeth Berg's novel, *The Year of Pleasures*:

> The world was full of cynicism and judgment and what I believed was a knee-jerk recoiling against sentimentality. What had happened to us that we sneered at expressions of

love and devoured stories of alienation and rage? Give me the hearts drawn on napkins, the men who walked on the street side of the sidewalk, the woman I met at a party who told me she always turned on Johnny Mathis to clean her bathroom. Give me the nurse who said, 'You know, people think I'm such a good person to do what I do. But they don't understand that I get far more than I give—it feels really good to take care of someone. It really does lift you up. When I go to work, I'm going to church.

I fought a low level of dread about all the work ahead and the apathy among secular reviewers my book would face, but I was fed up with the endless shaming and attacks lodged against us. The media lunged for any story that put the Orthodox in a bad light but never, ever explored the extraordinary good that thrived within these communities: The way they spontaneously and energetically rise up with meals and social, spiritual, and logistical support each time there is a person or family in distress. The networks of volunteer organizations that provide free loans of medical equipment, baby furniture, wedding gowns, money, civilian emergency medical services, and security details for Jewish neighborhoods increasingly vulnerable to anti-Semitic attacks—attacks largely greeted by the secular media with a yawn. The outpourings of prayers—personal and communal—to "storm the heavens" when individuals or communities are in danger or distress. These efforts are extraordinary and have no peer outside Jewish communities. Still, despite their novelty—or perhaps because of it—mainstream media ignores it all.

One evening, while still indulging in a little last-minute "To write, or not to write? That is the question?" musing, my friend David told me, "You ought to write this book even if it's only for your children's sake. They grew up religious. You didn't. It's important for them to learn about the life you lived before and how you came to this choice. It should inspire them and your grandchildren." Well, as much as I loved my kids, for all the work facing me I'd hope for an audience greater than four, but the time had come to stop dithering, roll up the proverbial sleeves, and start. Taking this on was part of the mission I had embraced years before and to which I remained wholeheartedly committed: to bring the Torah's timeless, uplifting truths into public awareness. I would do my best to tell the story of how I went from Berkely feminist to proud, independent-minded, Shabbat-observant woman to anyone willing to turn the pages. And I hoped to reach Jewish readers across the religious spectrum as well.

My life in a Torah-centered community had been filled with joys and sorrows, intellectual and spiritual stimulation and challenges, the unrivaled support and strength of community during difficult times, and the ongoing personal challenge of staying inspired. At times I had also been frustrated by "groupthink," sexism, and expectations to conform to community standards I did not like or understand. In my book I wrote honestly about my initial resistance to this journey, my awkward and embarrassing moments as a "newbie" Orthodox woman, and eventually, the personal growth path I began. Spiritual growth is not a place where you arrive; it's a lifelong journey. My memoir was as real as I could make it.

At first, I tried to write this book as I had my previous books—in between other writing and editing projects and family obligations. Soon, I saw this was impossible. This project required and deserved larger chunks of time, including time to simply sit and think. Once I allowed myself that space, the stories I wanted to write became clear. My confidence in my mission grew. As the book progressed, I tried to find a literary agent but soon gave up. Agents and traditional indie houses, overwhelmingly and sheeplike, were seeking fashionable fiction and nonfiction genres: nonbinary gender, young adult, issues involving race and class, and almost anything from "marginalized" voices. (You mean, marginalized like me?)

The publisher of She Writes Press, Brooke Warner, advertised her left-of-center politics prominently on social media, so I couldn't assume she would green-light my manuscript, but her company had a fantastic reputation, and I submitted my manuscript. It was fast-tracked in the system and *The Skeptic and the Rabbi: Falling in Love With Faith* was published in September 2017. I will always be grateful to Brooke, a longtime industry leader and champion of writers who are pursuing their publishing dreams, for her stalwart support.

Positive physical images of Orthodox Jews remained elusive among the stock photo image offerings, and I didn't like any of the cover designs presented to me. I was looking for something subtle: the suggestion of a woman turning toward faith. When I did my own search for images, even typing in any version of "women dressed modestly" or even "Orthodox Jewish women" brought up dozens of photos of Moslem women wearing the hijab. Not a single image of a Jewish woman with an attractive head scarf, hat or beret popped up. Varying my search terms, I eventually found my cover image: a woman seated against a wooden log, looking out toward a horizon of low hills carpeted in green against a dusky sunset. She is wearing a floppy burgundy hat (my favorite color) and a green sweater. Modestly dressed, the woman is clearly in a contemplative mood. I sent that image to my production manager and said: "This is it."

My memoir earned endorsements and accolades from notable Jewish educators and leaders and was reviewed generously where it was chosen for reviews. Notably, the Jewish Book Council, the clearinghouse for Jewish book reviews that had positively reviewed nearly every anti-Orthodox memoir, declined to review it. I remain heartened that readers continue to discover and enjoy *The Skeptic and the Rabbi*. Fortunately, several other baalei teshuva memoirs have been published since then, strengthening the genre.

At a speaking event discussing the memoir, a man raised his hand and asked, "If you were so enamored of a religious Jewish life, why didn't you want to become a rabbi? Don't you feel it's sexist that you can't become a rabbi?"

"This is a great question," I said, pleased by the challenge.

"The Torah wasn't written by the Equal Employment Opportunity Commission. God made it clear that it's in society's best interests for men to have certain public leadership roles. Even among Jewish men, roles are defined and limited by whether someone is a Kohein, a Levi, or a Yisrael. And Jewish women throughout history have carried enormous influence and had vital leadership roles."

I added that women's ordination among the more liberal denominations had not strengthened those movements, despite the undoubted capabilities and talents of the individual women themselves. There was still a stampede toward the exits in these congregations. I also acknowledged the problem of Jewish religious extremism, and general sexism in the Orthodox world. Most egregiously, many Jewish courts fail to aggressively confront husbands who refuse to give their estranged wives a *get*, or writ of Jewish divorce, leaving these women *agunot*, "chained" by Jewish law in dead marriages and unable to remarry. In more yeshivish or *hareidi* circles where I sometimes visit, the women's section in shuls is either so small or so visually cut off from the action on the men's side that I find it alienating. However, Orthodox Jewish women are in every profession imaginable, and increasingly are in leadership roles within schools, organizations, and communities. This trend only continues to grow.

"I'm most concerned with having impact through my life's work—not with having a title," I concluded. "The titles I have as wife, mother, daughter, sister, friend, community member, writer, and especially Jew, are more than enough for me."

Politics and the Writing World

*People say, "Oh, politics is so polarized today," and I'm thinking . . .
"1861, that was polarized."*
—P. J. O'Rourke

On June 25, 2009, I drove north toward Santa Barbara to a writers' conference. It wasn't often that I went to such conferences, but this event was tantalizingly close to home. Additionally, I would scoop up a modest award for some of my columns. Okay, "award" may be a stretch. My name would be announced as a winner in the humor category, and I would be presented with a small piece of paper attesting to this designation. I'd take that! I was especially pleased given that my submission package was comprised of columns that appeared on Jewish websites and newspapers.

One of the essays homed in on the multiple indignities of modern airline travel, such as surrendering your valuables into a plastic tub that sails away on a conveyer belt while you stand around in your socks and TSA agents stare at grainy images of your personal belongings, whispering to colleagues about what they guess those belongings suggest about your private habits. As a kosher traveler I had an extra complaint:

> In London, security agents confiscated our peanut butter and our jelly. In Cincinnati my yogurt was seized, no doubt because of the "active cultures" lurking inside. . . On our recent jaunt to Albuquerque, just as we were about to reach

for our shoes and reclaim some semblance of our dignity, the conveyer belt was sent in reverse. Predictably, one agent had second thoughts about our food bag. I began to wonder what it was with these TSA agents and food. They seemed obsessed with it. Didn't these people get lunch breaks? Two agents stared intently into the x-ray machine screen. They furrowed their brows, pointed fingers, and shook their heads.

A majordomo from the TSA poked and prodded our kosher eats, and I don't think he was looking for the kosher hechshers, either. Other than saturated fat in the Danish, I felt our foodstuffs were both patriotic and safe. After riffling through our sandwiches, a container of hummus, two apples, a wilting cheese stick, and the divine chocolate Danish, he finally unearthed a large plastic frozen ice pack, inspecting it from a distance, as if he thought it might contain explosives. *It's an ice pack, not an ice pick*, I wanted to argue, but knowing how often they mistake short Caucasian women for Islamic terrorists, I kept my mouth shut. (from "Shoeless in Albuquerque," published on Aish.com.)

I had never won a journalism award before and was eager to savor the moment—well, fifteen seconds, anyway—when I could bask in the modest glory among a cadre of about 150 fellow columnists. Several notable speakers were also scheduled during the program, including Jeffrey Zaslow, one of my favorite columnists from the *Wall Street Journal*, who died just three years later in a tragic car accident. As I drove, the radio was broadcasting endless and frenzied reporting of the death of Michael Jackson, announced that morning. In addition to speculation about possible causes of death of the music superstar, reporters hit the streets to record the hysterical grief among Jackson's fans.

Jackson had been phenomenally talented, but increasingly bizarre, given his penchant for sleepovers with young children. Just who were these parents who sent their kids to stay overnight in Neverland with this ghostly apparition? The mind reels. Journalists would squeeze this news for as much public anguish as possible. Tomorrow they'd need a new disaster, or, lacking a true catastrophe, something they could gin up and inflate to disaster status. The coverage was almost clinically overwrought, yet I couldn't pull myself away from its creepiness. Sobbing fans spoke as if the world had ended, as if we had lost Mother Theresa. Our society had a harder time distinguishing between fame and moral significance. Poor Michael Jackson—perhaps that level of celebrity could make almost anyone lose their grip on reality.

When I arrived at the hotel, I looked forward to schmoozing with other writers, but it didn't take long for politics to intrude. As a member of several writers' and editors' organizations, I had always been inspired by the spirited camaraderie and unwavering encouragement that so many people working in a fiercely competitive industry offered to one another. Most of us were freelancers with no job security. Bread-and-butter clients could suddenly have a change in management, direction, or heart, leaving a big hole in monthly income. Digital media continued to decimate print media, with thousands of previously steady writing opportunities disappearing, and writers were scrambling to pivot to nonwriting jobs or other "content creation." Wherever we were in our writerly journeys, each of us jockeying for position in a rapidly changing market, the congregation of fellow and sister scribes unfailingly offered support, suggestions, and friendship.

Living in a thriving Jewish community where most of my social connections were also Shabbat-observant, it was important to me to maintain as broad a professional network as possible. Through our online discussions, I learned from writers who had expertise on all kinds of topics and through this network, I kept up with industry trends. Occasionally I had something to contribute to conversations from my own experiences and knowledge. I especially liked joining the annual holiday gift exchange and mailing a Christmas gift to a colleague and signing my card, "From your Secret Santa!"

However, as kind and supportive as this community was, their views were almost uniformly left-of-center, and they didn't cotton much to differing views. Moderators warned members to avoid political topics except for one discussion board reserved for the subject. Still, political views seeped into the career-focused conversations. For example, mentions of a writer's newly published op-ed or interview with a notable figure invariably referred to those published in politically left newspapers (an almost redundant term) or magazines. It also showed up when writers fished for suggestions about whom to interview or how to contact a desirable interview subject for a topic whose leftist angle had already been baked into the topic. This was all par for the course, mirroring what I read and heard in the news media every day on NPR, in the *Los Angeles Times, New York Times*, and through other legacy media channels.

I warned myself to STAY OUT of the political discussion group, but like an addict, I couldn't help but wander into the bar, pull up a stool, and order a drink. I found spirited debates fun and hoped to engage in some respectful tussles. These point-counterpoint debates of robust and even heated quality used to be normal in our society, including in newspaper columns and television news shows, but had become increasingly rare. Nor did I want to live in an ideological bubble. Closing ourselves off to opinions we disagree with also closes our minds and promotes intolerance.

I found, though, that no matter the issue, whether proposed legislation about immigration, child health insurance, or the next presidential race, only one or two others agreed with my point of view. The rest of the regulars in this forum disagreed only on tactics to get the job done. These were passionate, sometimes zealous, individuals. Politics for them was religion, leftism their orthodoxy. This was no forum for debate; it was just a feel-good echo chamber where ideological interlopers were quickly made to feel the error of their views, which not too many years earlier would have been considered moderate but were now slammed as right-wing, or sometimes, fascist.

Having waded into unfriendly territory, I looked for any point of agreement possible and made sure to acknowledge the good intentions of the other members. However, whenever I'd present what I considered compelling, reliable evidence for my point of view, unless that evidence came from a left-of-center source, they ridiculed it. They saw no difference between an article from a respected journal such as *National Review* versus the rantings of some blogger stockpiling canned goods for the end times from a remote cabin in Utah.

I asked myself, "Are you just as close-minded to their views as they are to yours? How can we find any common ground?" This was an important question. We had become a society of outrage, dangerously polarized. However, a key difference between these other writers and the tiny handful of us who held moderate or right-of-center views was that we listened to and read from their "acceptable" sources as well as our own all the time. We could compare coverage from the *Los Angeles Times* and NPR versus the *Spectator, National Review,* or *Commentary*. They contemptuously dismissed reporting and commentary from nonleft sources, but I doubted that any of them had ever—or would ever—even give these other sources a chance.

Occasionally I'd get emails or private messages from lurkers in the group who shared my perspective. "I admire you for taking them on," wrote Julie. "I think you're very brave, but I can't afford to publicize my views in this community." Self-censoring was a real growth industry among this group of "diversity-loving," "radically inclusive" progressives.

Judaism teaches that we give everyone the benefit of the doubt, which helped me do the same for these writers with whom I disagreed so strongly. It also teaches the value of staying silent in the face of rebuke or insult. Both lessons helped me try to be as fair as I thought I could be in my exchanges. I also learned to fight my nature and say nothing in response on the rare occasion when I was insulted, such as the time when a longtime, formerly very friendly leftist colleague suddenly accused me of "gaslighting." At the time, I wasn't even sure of what the term meant, and I had to look it up. It was a despicable accusation, and I felt my heart thudding in my chest. This colleague had been so warm and friendly up till then. I felt gut-punched and bewildered, and it took me a few days to recover from the shock of it. I instantly cut off all connection with this person without a word of response.

Not standing up for myself or confronting the attacker didn't come naturally to me. I'm not one to back down from a fight, but I understood that the Jewish approach was the only wise—or even sane—course. Eventually, I got worn down by these fruitless discussions, and after one too many rhetorical hangovers I was cured from going back into that bar and ordering another drink. I was close to getting cirrhosis of the liberal.

Coming out of the closet as a conservative exacted a cost. My social stock value—such as it was—began to fall even among the larger group as a whole, whose members probably poked their heads in the political forum for a look-see. This became noticeable particularly on Facebook, where I had amassed well over 150 "friends" just from writing circles. Naturally, we shared news of our published work, and as good social media citizens do, often posted supportive comments or at least clicked the "like" button—a grossly overvalued currency. I'm embarrassed to admit that I was bothered, even hurt, that I earned almost none of these cheap affirmations from this group when I posted links to my work, even when the articles were completely apolitical, such as columns about holidays, parenting, or friendship. With so little in common with most of these writers and feeling marginalized, I "unfriended" most of them, keeping only those who continued to share gracious exchanges with me.

I felt the loss of connection much more acutely with true friends. As I had predicted years earlier when I had begun my Jewish journey, friendships from my younger years began to fade. Geographical distance was part of the equation, but the greater, unbridgeable distance was in our diverging religious, cultural, and political views. This happens to many relationships over time; friendships do fade or die of natural causes. Still, it shocked me when one day I clicked on "Haley's" Facebook page to see that she had replaced her personal photo—where she stood next to her husband, both of them smiling—with an illustration aiming daggers at political conservatives. This high-voltage image was of Lady Liberty, blindfolded and forcibly held down on a table. A man stands above her menacingly, his white hands projecting out of the sleeves of an expensive-looking suit. He clamps one hand over her mouth; the other immobilizes her wrist, as Lady Liberty's scales of justice lay in disarray. To avoid any uncertainty about who the villain is, the abuser's shirt cuffs are burnished with the bold red, white, and blue Republican elephant logo.

I gaped at the illustration, feeling a small tear in my heart. Haley and I had been close for more than twenty-five years. She was delightful, adventurous, smart, warm, and funny, and I admired her as well as loved her. She was the friend I called immediately and through my tears told her that the guy I had fallen madly in love with during my freshman year in college had just told me, "It's over." Our lively and intimate friendship remained solid year after year. Eventually, she was the only friend I still had from adolescence, the others having drifted away, making the connection one of my most cherished. During college I had introduced her to a friend of mine, thinking they would make a great couple. I was honored to be a witness at their wedding.

Like Haley, I used to wear my liberal identity as a badge of honor, a statement of my moral virtue and sophistication. When I met Jeff and first listened to his religious and political viewpoints, my heart began to race. I liked how I perceived the world, and if I discovered that Jeff might be right, at least about certain things, my whole sense of identity would be thrown into a tailspin. I might have to *change*. But then I realized that if I refused to even *listen* to Jeff's views, which were new to me, my liberalism was a fraud. And I was a journalist—shouldn't I be curious about "the other side of the story?" I listened—grudgingly—looking for opportunities to argue about theology and politics. Naturally, I found plenty. But I also began to read prominent conservative thinkers, such as Dennis Prager, Michael Medved, George Will, Charles Krauthammer, Peggy Noonan, Norman Podhoretz, Ruth Wisse, and others. It was impossible not to be wowed by their intellectual clarity, knowledge of history, and the damaging fallout from social and political progressivism that they traced with pinpoint accuracy. I cared about truth, and realized the liberals didn't own the concept of compassion. I saw that in fact, many progressive policies were actually regressive and oppressive.

As my religious world expanded to embrace traditional Jewish values, so too did my political views begin to list rightward in the face of new, irrefutable data and patterns. Releasing my fiercely protected identity as an enlightened liberal was very difficult. But over time, it was easier for me to just let go of that emotional connection to liberalism, thinking, "I don't need you anymore."

Haley and I maintained our friendship for several years even after my life and beliefs had begun to change, finding common ground in talking about our families, work, books, music, and more. It worked, sort of, but I'm certain we both sensed a small undercurrent of tension from the foundational shift in my life. As time went on, the unspoken gap between our worldviews distanced us further, as it had with other friends. After I posted a link on Facebook to an article demonstrating that tighter gun control laws didn't correlate with lower rates of gun violence, a mutual friend of Haley's and mine typed a frosty retort: "The Judy I knew used to be more nuanced." *Ouch!* The accusation of "lack of nuance" was one of the sharpest daggers in a liberal's arsenal.

Haley's choice to fuse her political and personal personae on social media was upsetting for an additional reason. Politics was becoming increasingly divisive, rupturing countless relationships, including in families. The illustration she posted was inked with vitriol, and with its implied sexual violence, it cheapened the experience of women who had endured such trauma.

Ironies abounded in this situation. Plenty of men on the left had been guilty of or strongly associated with sexual exploitation and abuse, including presidents, governors, senators, Hollywood producers, and other "notables." And wasn't it conservative speakers who were frequently threatened with violence if they dared speak on college campuses, where students threatened to feel "unsafe" if these speakers were allowed to articulate their views? Spineless administrators caved in to these threats and even encouraged them, endorsing their students' fragility. Many speakers' invitations were cancelled, and outrageous, threatening disruptions of other presentations were tolerated. Leftists not only already dominated college campuses, but also most news outlets, and social media platforms, including Google, Twitter/X, and YouTube, whose hoodie-wearing foot soldiers censored and restricted access to content they deemed "disinformation" (but much of which later was revealed to be true).

Who exactly was gagging whom?

The conceit that views from the left were morally superior—and *normal*—showed itself throughout society, and the writers' conference was no exception. Table conversations volubly got political, with no thought that anyone who might be at the table might think differently. I had chosen to sit next to Karen, the only colleague at the event who I knew for certain also held politically conservative views. When speakers at the podium offered barbed jokes that scorched Republicans not just politically but in ad hominem attacks, Karen raised an eyebrow at me, while we both tried to suppress smiles. A columnist from a large Texas daily who knew my views rushed over from another table, knelt down next to me, and started fanning me in exaggerated fashion, asking, "Are you okay?" Dave was a really nice guy and I saw that he was only half-joking, in no way mocking me. I appreciated his gesture and assured him I wouldn't collapse.

This was a writers' conference. Why weren't we having a knock-down, drag-out argument about the Oxford comma? Or debating the ethics of using editing or story-writing software? Finding new paying outlets for our work? It was no different anywhere else in secular writing and publishing circles. Both the Authors Guild and the Medill School of Journalism each published snippy essays in their magazines vilifying talk radio, which was code for "conservative." Paradoxically, the Authors Guild president's message warned that "tolerance is not ascendant in our national life today. It's intolerance that sells, drawing listeners to talk radio and viewers to cable news networks." But he himself had no tolerance for the genre as a whole nor shared any evidence of its dangers. He didn't offer any theory as to why liberal hosts kept flopping miserably in the exact same show format.

A more bellicose essay published in the Medill alumni magazine referred to all of talk radio as "right-wing extremist," holding a "monopoly" over the genre made possible by "conservatives with big bankrolls" who hired "syndicated yellers planted by ideologues." I wrote rebuttals to both essays, asking why people concerned with "fairness" and "tolerance" on the airwaves didn't concern themselves with lack of balance on network news, PBS, and NPR, where the chance of hearing a conservative view on issues of politics and culture was about as likely as getting hit by lightning. To their credit, both magazines published my rebuttals in full.

But the hard-left direction of the media world was a runaway train. In May 2020, when widespread protests and riots broke out during heavy COVID lockdowns after the murder of George Floyd by Minneapolis police officer Derek Chauvin, the Editorial Freelancers Association rushed out a statement standing in solidarity with the protesters. This was the first time since I'd joined the EFA years earlier that they had ever taken any overt political stand. Given the chaos and violence, as well as their repeated concern for members over COVID safety, I was appalled.

I wrote a letter asking the leadership why they couldn't spare a scrap of sympathy for business owners whose storefronts were smashed and looted (often in minority communities), for the rampaging destruction of public and private property, the nihilistic violence targeting innocent citizens, police cars set on fire, and for police offers injured or even killed trying to maintain order. Among them was Black retired police captain David Dorn, murdered while trying to protect his friend's St. Louis pawn shop during the chaos that media outfits kept insisting were "mostly peaceful protests."

These folks were in the business of communication and listening, even offering seminars for editors wanting to learn how to get work as "sensitivity readers," but my email was met with the silence of those who brook no dissent. Two weeks later, I sent it again, making sure it had been received. Finally, they curtly acknowledged receipt without further comment. No explanation for their having suddenly politicized the EFA in such an extraordinary and partisan way. They talked a good game about elevating "marginalized" voices into the public conversation, but their inability or unwillingness to even acknowledge the existence of a minority voice in their midst proved their shameful and mindless conformity.

Similarly, I found the Poynter Institute, an organization that "champions freedom of expression, civil dialogue, and compelling journalism that helps citizens participate in healthy democracies," exclusively champions left-of-center media coverage. After enrolling in an advanced editing certificate program through Poynter, I began receiving their daily email digests, which included commentary about media coverage of people and issues in the news. Notably, they ignored emerging stories that revealed how the media's lockstep political bias had created misleading and false coverage on many issues, including the claims of Russian collusion in the Trump presidential campaign and that the damning evidence on Hunter Biden's laptop was part of that conspiracy.

Though Poynter also claims to "prepare journalists worldwide to hold powerful people accountable and promote honest information in the marketplace of ideas," they had no interest in holding powerful people in the media accountable for false, sloppy, or agenda-driven coverage. I pointed out specific glaring omissions and evidence of their bias in two emails to the editor of the daily digest. But the marketplace of ideas was closed, and I never heard back.

I also stopped renewing my dues to the Authors Guild. They did vital work in supporting and protecting authors' rights, from fair contracts to copyright protection and more. I had personally benefited from their legal advice on a publishing contract and had attended worthwhile seminars. But they lost me when they went for woke with Puritanical zeal.

The Guild's toadying over the banner of diversity, equity, and inclusion (DEI) had become tedious and tendentious, but my breaking point came from their hysteria over the issue of so-called banned books. Many school boards and some state legislatures had ramped up efforts to keep certain books out of school and community libraries, many of which were sexually explicit LGBTQ memoirs and novels aimed at a youth audience. For example, the memoir "Gender Queer" often required parental consent for readers under eighteen.

In breathless emails to its membership over this threat, the AG coyly made sure to mention classic modern literature that some parents objected to, such as Kurt Vonnegut's *Slaughterhouse-Five* and Margaret Atwood's *The Handmaid's Tale,* but not *This Book Is Gay, Out of Darkness,* and *We Are the Ants,* all of which include explicit sexual content. No library can stock every book, and school libraries in particular need to respect community standards and consider what is age- and theme-appropriate for children. Not carrying a book in a library doesn't ban it. All these books were readily available for purchase online.

This anxiety over "banned books" actually camouflages the truth: the left loves the public relations bonanzas they reap from fearmongering over the prospect of banned books to an alarmed public. Banned Books Week has been celebrated annually since 1982, and "brings together the entire book community—librarians, booksellers, publishers, journalists, teachers, and readers of all types—in shared support of the freedom to seek and to express ideas, even those some consider unorthodox or unpopular," according to their website.

Ever the cantankerous correspondent, I got busy writing a letter to the Authors Guild about their false narrative and was pleased to receive an invitation to discuss it with CEO Mary Rasenberger. During our Zoom call, I challenged the organization's framing of the issue as a "ban," which I felt was deeply dishonest in the context of current events.

"'Ban' might not have been the best word to describe it," Rasenberger acknowledged. "It's something I will bring up at a future meeting with board members."

I also asked why the Guild had shown no similar outrage over a much closer attempt at a book ban over Abigail Shrier's courageous book, *Irreversible Damage: The Transgender Craze Seducing Our Daughters*, published in 2020.

"Shrier's book was refused reviews and advertising space by Amazon and yanked from the shelves at Target in response to two Twitter rants," I explained, and the American Booksellers Association fell on its sword apologizing to members for the "serious, violent incident" of sending a paperback copy of Shrier's book to them. As I spoke, I saw Rasenberger looking something up on her computer. "I'm totally against efforts like this, but I hadn't heard about it," she said. Given how well publicized the situation had been, this was a stunning admission.

"Maybe efforts to cancel writers with conservative views aren't considered any real threat to free speech," I said. "The Guild should know about them and respond with equal vigor to attacks against conservative writers."

During our meeting, Rasenberger seemed a bit distracted and uncomfortable, but how could I blame her? I was my most polite self but would take no prisoners during my one chance for an audience with the Guild's top executive. Though I knew my arguments wouldn't budge the organization from its lockstep obedience to the DEI and LGBTQ agenda, dialogue with people with whom you disagreed on substantive social issues was in short supply these days. Overall, it was a healthy conversation, and I appreciated her willingness to speak with me.

I couldn't help but wonder if anyone at the Authors Guild saw the connection between the wildly out of proportion number of books for teens—and increasingly, very young children—that stimulate confusion about sexual identity and the skyrocketing rates of kids with anxiety and depression. Books are written in order to inform, inspire, and persuade. How could they refuse to even consider a connection between the two simultaneous trends? Mental health outcomes for those who did transition were often worse than for those who didn't. And a rising tide of young adults were speaking out about having been rushed into transitioning, which they now believe had ruined their lives. So how was this push really working out for everybody?

And what about the reading market of millions of teens who are heterosexual and have traditional views? Didn't those readers also crave understanding—perhaps now more than ever? Didn't they also deserve to see relatable literary protagonists on the page?

As the industry became hopelessly stifling, my enthusiasm to be a minor player in this community of writers withered. It was frustrating. I had enjoyed my connections and conversations with writers who were unlike me religiously, geographically, and in terms of topic knowledge. It was stimulating and healthy, socially and intellectually. But politics had become a suffocating, soggy blanket that infected nearly every interaction and had bled into continuing education courses for writers and editors. And so I retreated, holding onto a handful of relationships with writers who had not let their politics intrude in online or social media discussions.

If not for my natural optimism and the optimism that is taught by my faith, I would have become cynical and bitter over the lockstep bias from editors and publishers who had no interest in publishing material that reflected traditional religion in a positive light—even if it was "my lived experience" and "my truth"—those supposed literary lodestars. Holocaust novels and memoirs were still in demand, though. As Dara Horn observed acerbically through the title of her 2021 book, *People Love Dead Jews*.

More Blessings

Who is wise? He who learns from every person. Who is strong? He who subdues his personal inclinations. Who is rich? He who is happy with his lot.
—Ethics of the Fathers 4:1

During this period, I often recalled my emotional meeting with Rachel, that wise and empathic teacher of Jewish spirituality, who had asked me the crystallizing question, "Where is the blessing coming from in your work?" Since I had met with her several years before, my professional blessings had multiplied from a wellspring of Jewish sources. At long last, I had as steady a workflow in writing and editing as I wanted. I had sought acceptance into the bigger world of writers and editors, hoping to find a sense of inclusion. And while I was grateful for the handful of colleagues with whom I maintained very friendly relationships—despite our differing politics—in any group or communal setting (including online discussions) I found a resounding intellectual claustrophobia, groupthink, and prejudice.

Feeling a bit like Dorothy in the final scene of *The Wizard of Oz*, I found that "there's no place like home." After years of struggle, I had accepted that every element in my life, from my personal circumstances to my professional achievements, was meant for me. I believed all my challenges and blessings were sent from God to help me fulfill my mission on Earth. Admittedly, some days this was a struggle, but most days, this felt real—and liberating.

I hadn't been raised to see life as an unfurling of God's gifts or messages. I gained this "sight" after having opened myself up to the possibilities of a Torah-based life in a community that valued independent, creative thinking. It was a community that respected the roads that we baalei teshuva had traveled. Rabbi Lapin did not view our previous actions or lifestyles as dreadful moral errors to be ashamed of (though many of us carried a lot of regret for past behaviors), but part of a life journey that had been necessary to bring us to this point. We brought our distinct talents, insights, and experiences that shot creative energy into our new lives and communities. With this assurance, it didn't take long for me to realize that the more I chose to see God in my life, the more strikingly I felt His presence. If I considered events to be random or happenstance, they *would* become random or happenstance. But the stronger my awareness and feeling of security that God is my friend and that we have a relationship, the wider He opens that door, guiding my steps. Perception creates reality.

Through my Jewish professional network, I learned of a Hasidic rabbi who was working on a self-help book. He had gone through two writers who had disappointed him and was now shopping for a third. Given his religious social boundaries, he requested that only men apply for the assignment.

Within three minutes, I had emailed him, briefly outlining my credentials and offering a complimentary partial edit. I didn't need to announce my pronouns for him to realize I was female, and in my mind I dared him to respond. He did, and based on my sample edit he hired me. Given that Yiddish was the rabbi's primary language, I sometimes felt a little *farmisht* (confused) and needed to ask several questions before I was *farshteyn* (clear) on his *kevana* (meaning), but we worked well together. He was completely self-taught in psychology, and I found his theories insightful and compelling. In fact, I recognized several people I knew who fit his description of what he called an "ultraviolet" personality, whose trademark characteristic was an exceptional, unsustainable degree of emotional fragility.

I shook my head in disbelief at the sloppy mess the last writer had left behind, rewrote much of the book and helped my client choose a self-publishing option. The feminist in me silently harrumphed that my work was far superior to that of the male editors he had previously hired. I also respected him for breaking beyond his comfort zone to work with me. He was an appreciative, *erliche kleyent* (upstanding client) who paid my invoices within minutes. I know his book has helped thousands of people.

I also ghostwrote a primer on Jewish ethics and philosophy, a fulfilling project that deepened my own religious education and fit the type of "mission work" I felt so well suited for. I added Torah passages here and there to underscore the author's lessons, something I could never have done years earlier when I was still a newbie baalas teshuva and knew so little about Jewish teachings. In this particular assignment, I had no direct contact with the author, who had no idea who was actually writing his book. Spiritually, I understood that it was healthy for me to be a silent partner, another exercise in taming my ego. And yet, as Golda Meir once said, "Don't be humble. You're not that great." I decided that invisibility was a nice place to visit but I wouldn't want to live there.

For a while, rabbis seemed to become specialty clients. For more than one year I worked with Rabbi Gershon Schusterman on his book *Why, God, Why? How To Believe in Heaven When It Hurts Like Hell.* This client knew his subject because he had lived it. The rabbi's first wife, Rochel Leah, died suddenly at age thirty-six, leaving him a widower with eleven children to raise—the youngest sixteen-month-old twins. As a day school director who had been raised and educated in the Chabad-Lubavitch community, Rabbi Schusterman was blindsided by his loss. The theologically based answers he normally offered to the bereaved now felt alarmingly flat.

For thirty years, Rabbi Schusterman had wanted to write this book. Finally, with his children grown and no longer running a school, he drafted it with the guidance of another experienced writer. By the time it was in my hands, he hoped it only needed a bit of editorial dusting off. I saw things differently, urging him to share more of his personal story and struggle with faith. I also encouraged him to give more prominence to his second wife, Chana Rachel, who helped him raise his children and who was instrumental in his healing. It was an honor to have earned his trust, and we developed a close collaboration, both of us excited to watch his manuscript really shine with a more personal tone as well as additional context and clarity.

This project began to feel very personal to me, no doubt because of my own family's experience reeling from tragedy decades earlier. Rabbi Schusterman put forth compelling evidence based on Jewish sources that the soul lives eternally, as he also outlined a psychologically sophisticated path from initial grief and anger to a hopeful, optimistic future. These reassuring ideas had only been introduced to me when I began my Jewish journey as an adult. Working with Rabbi Schusterman felt like a gift from God, a project that nourished me professionally and personally.

When the time came to determine a first print run, I cautioned him to have modest expectations. "Your book is wonderful and valuable, but the marketplace is filled with books that offer spiritual comfort after loss. I would hate for you to be sitting on cases and cases of unsold books," I said, suggesting a small initial print run of only 2,000 copies. Fortunately, this time Rabbi Schusterman did not listen to me. He ordered a print run of 4,000, which sold out within four months, a superb showing for a book without the backing of even a midsized publisher. Thousands of readers who needed his message responded immediately through emails and online reviews.

As one reader posted online, "After the initial shock of a recent personal loss, I was angry at God. Why was this happening to me?! I am good, I am kind, I am caring and always try to do the right thing and I have been through enough! From the excruciating pain I was experiencing I was starting to sink into depression. Fortunately, friends gave me Rabbi Schusterman's book . . . [it] gave me comfort and strength. It restored my hope and enabled me to recommit to my life and its purpose."

At one of Rabbi Schusterman's first book signings, the room was packed with more than eighty people, nearly all of whom were clutching a signed copy (if not two or three) by the end of the evening. To know that I had a hand in shaping this book and helping to spread the author's message of comfort rivaled, if not exceeded, the satisfaction I had enjoyed from any of my solo efforts.

Throwing myself into book editing projects brought me great professional joy. I cared about each author and their book, Jewish or not. I assured each author (except the one who didn't know I was writing his book) that I was there to offer support, helping them communicate their message to their intended audience in their authentic voice. When they would get frustrated or fatigued during the process, I promised that together we'd eventually reach the promised land of a sparkling manuscript that they could be proud of.

Editing and coaching balanced out the intensity of my own writing. I still felt an almost feverish need to write. Too-long stretches between writing sessions resulted in grumpiness. I needed to write when I was in a good mood. I needed to write when anxious or distressed. Sometimes I was amazed that during times of extreme worry or turmoil, I could knock out some pretty funny satire, unsure of where it bubbled up from but making myself laugh out loud during the process. (Of course, this could also have merely indicated that I was losing my mind from worry.) One of the spiritual mentors I consulted with on occasion reassured me that my need to write wasn't selfish: "Creativity is energy," he told me, as I sighed in relief. Writing was also cathartic. For me, it has always been as elemental as breathing, a way to find meaning, hope, and laughter in a complicated world.

Column Fodder on Aisle 9!

Write your heart out.
—Joyce Carol Oates, *The Faith of a Writer*

Still in love with writing after so many years, I refused to become cozy or complacent with my skill level. With each new essay or feature story, I was eager and often excited to see how I would take the unformed clay of an idea and refine, shape, define, and give it contour and color. This was a continual process that involved thinking and much revising until it was time to let go and submit for publication. When I noticed that my vocabulary began to seem slightly predictable—at least to me—I renewed my practice, begun decades earlier, of making lists of words I came across while reading that would jazz things up a bit. One list that grew briskly included the words *inscrutable, docile, gushing, venerable, callow, impassable,* and *mirthful.* None were new words, but I still wrote them down as part of practice to add sparkle to my craft. The English language is incredibly rich, with boundless potential for literary expansion. For inspiration, I read fiction and nonfiction, humor and history, Torah glosses and political commentary. Vocabulary diversity—the struggle is real!

Feature writing required "workmanlike" journalism skills, but I loved the essay form above all others. A very fine essay is a work of art, and I sometimes envied writers who were able to broaden their life experiences through travel and write about them. Alas, my lifestyle doesn't allow for African safaris, touring the El Yunque

Rain Forest in Puerto Rico, or zipping over to the archipelago islands of Fiji, so I have always looked for essay material in life's prosaic, everyday moments. Many of these moments have occurred in the grocery store. As COVID and national hysteria were both breaking out simultaneously in March 2020, I wrote a satirical piece called "Buddy, Can You Spare a Chicken?" about the hoarding I'd seen at a local kosher store two weeks before Passover:

> Standing in a line twelve people deep, I coveted my neighbor's chickens. This tiny, elderly woman presided over a cart that runneth over with tantalizingly fresh poultry, enough to last her through Pesach 2025. My frozen fowl was of indeterminate vintage, but beggars can't be choosers. In vain, I struggled not to judge her irrational, seemingly selfish buying. She should live and be well. Sporting events may have been canceled for now, but this was truly March Madness: ruthless competitive shopping, a survival of the fastest. Where was my Xanax when I needed it?

About a year later, at a large grocery chain store where I shopped regularly, I was moved by an encounter with the checkout clerk, a Black man I had never seen before. His name tag read Emeka, and he exuded a vibrant optimism and charisma. From behind the Plexiglass barrier, I asked him how he pronounced his name, which led to my column, "An Encounter of Hope in the Grocery Store."

"My name is pronounced 'e-MEH-kah.' It means 'what God has done is good' in Nigerian." He spoke with pride, "a dignified man," I wrote. While scanning the bar codes on my nectarines, asparagus, milk, and crackers, Emeka told me about coming here from Nigeria and the successful life he had built. He owned a home, his wife worked as a healthcare professional, and their three children excelled in school. "America is the land of opportunity!" he boasted with a smile. I was disappointed when my purchase was complete because

I was enjoying hearing this special individual talk. I told Emeka I looked forward to seeing him again.

"God bless you!" he said, and I returned the blessing in full. I ended the column with this observation:

> This little encounter in the market should not have been notable. But with racially charged protests and riots plaguing many cities, everyday encounters between people of color and Whites assume an outsized significance. That made my fleeting connection with Emeka healing, uplifting, even moving. In a time of depressing social and political strife, I will long cherish this beautiful moment, one made possible by a shared outlook of faith in God.

Even the most exciting essay sale of my career (other than my first-ever sale when I was twenty-two) sprang—or perhaps more accurately, danced—out of a visit to the gym I had been attending for years. This West Hollywood studio was hilariously self-conscious about creating an atmosphere it described on its website as "affirmatively productive, positive, and helpful. Our clients are given all the tools necessary for personal transformation. Spread love!"

There was just one problem: many dance classes at this otherwise exquisitely sensitive gym were taught against a backdrop of obscene, violent, misogynistic lyrics that referred to women as bitches and hos. This was anything but affirmatively productive, positive, or helpful. It hurt my chakras something awful. I half expected the little Buddha statue at the entrance door to stick his fat fingers in his ears when the instructor pressed the *play* button.

I wrote an essay about this atmospheric disconnect and submitted it to the *Wall Street Journal*—my dream publication. Previous submissions had all been rejected, but I smelled success inching closer when I began to receive personal notes from the commentary page editor encouraging me to try again, instead of the standard, unsigned email acknowledging receipt of my submission followed by the silence of rejection.

I knew that this essay, "Too Many Reps to Raunchy Music Hurts My Core," was perfect for the WSJ. But when I didn't hear anything several days after submission, my mood darkened. If I couldn't sell this, I would give up on them entirely. But then, five days after submission, I received an email early in the morning with a subject line of, "Good news from the Wall Street Journal." I snidely assumed it was from the marketing department offering a discount if I renewed my subscription early and nearly deleted it without even reading it. My better instincts told me to click and read. I did. Then I read it again. And again. The email was from Bari Weiss, then an editor at the paper, saying they were buying my piece and running it the next day—in the weekend edition. Would I be around to discuss edits that morning?

I was nearly dizzy with elation. Could I be hallucinating? I wondered. That's how badly I had wanted to break through to this market. After I agreed to the few minor edits Bari had suggested, I called Jeff, my voice cracking with uncontrollable excitement, then texted all the kids to tell them that Mom had hit the essay jackpot. I spent the day in a daze, shopping and cooking for Shabbat, but I don't recall burning anything or pouring salt into the cake batter instead of sugar.

The next morning, the *Wall Street Journal* sat on our walkway as usual in its sealed plastic slip. And there it lay all day and all afternoon, until Shabbat had officially ended. Our observance of Shabbat precluded us from bringing in the newspaper or the mail until after the holy day ended. To distract myself, I went to shul, where a few friends who did bring in their paper had read the story and told me how much they enjoyed it. I felt better: it really was there! The second I knew Shabbat was over, I dashed outside to grab the paper, tearing open the sleeve even before I was back in the house. I laid it open on the dining room table and as quickly as my fingers could fly, opened to the page before the main editorials—where freelance commentaries appear. There it was: my story, my byline in the *Journal*. This was a personal best for me, one that had taken many years to achieve. My piece read, in part:

> People today have become obsessed with physical sensitivities. We don't use paper towels; we don't smoke in public; we ask dinner guests about their dietary restrictions. We even eschew sending our kids to school with peanut-butter sandwiches because of the harmful physical impact it might have on others. But meanwhile we have lost our sensitivity to the things that pollute us spiritually, including entertainment that is often profoundly dark, violent, and misogynistic.
>
> Until I find a gym that demonstrates equal sensitivity to my inner core as much as my abdominal one, I am working out at home to DVDs and YouTube videos. My old gym owner ought to be proud: after all, I'm reducing my carbon footprint by not driving back and forth to the gym. Taking deep, cleansing breaths during exercise, as I was taught to do at the gym, is also easier in my living room because I no longer have to anticipate hearing Robin Thicke or Rihanna singing inane, nihilistic songs that may have great beats, but coarsen the soul. Besides, in the world to come I hear there's no pressure to look good in Spandex.

I'd still love to go to Fiji one day, or that writer's retreat in Tuscany, but you don't have to travel far to find things to write about. My writing canvas is expansive, covering relationships, history, humor, community issues, personality profiles, book reviews, and ideas, all through a lens of Jewish identity and values.

Still Navigating the Joyful Chaos of Working from Home

When I stand before God at the end of my life, I would hope that I would not have a single bit of talent left, and could say, "I used everything you gave me."
—Erma Bombeck

One Sunday afternoon I served my go-to sour cream coffee cake at a family celebration. This recipe is always a hit, greeted with big smiles and forks poised with enthusiasm. This time, however, the cake literally did not—could not—rise to the occasion. Not only had I omitted at least one key ingredient—the sour cream, and probably the baking soda—but I had been trying to bake with five young grandchildren underfoot, three of whom had insisted on helping. I should have left the whole thing to my granddaughters, seven and nine, who were already veteran bakers.

However, I wanted to bake with the girls while somehow also watching over three rambunctious boys, ages five, four, and two. These were several distractions too far. Sadly, the cake paid the ultimate penalty. Luckily, Gruens aren't picky when it comes to cake. With enough flour, oil, sugar, and chocolate, we are very forgiving, even of this flattened pancake, buried under an avalanche of confetti sprinkles, courtesy of a four-year-old baker in training.

I love these Sundays and the joyful chaos they bring—culinary and otherwise. My love for my family is boundless, my satisfaction to have such blessings profound. In a time when so many young adults are questioning or putting off marriage and families, I realize I live with an embarrassment of riches. But even basking in the glow of my family, I admit that after a few hours, my thoughts begin to wander to my writing work in process. As Jeff and I finish cleaning up after our kids and their spouses sweep our grandchildren back into the minivans, I am thinking of anecdotes, ideas, and phrases that I hope will arrest my readers' interest. I am keen to get the words on paper the following day.

My need to write is deeply ingrained, something that chose me more than I chose it, and as essential to me as breathing. When one of my wise advisors told me years earlier that creativity is energy, I wrote down that phrase and taped it to my computer. It encourages me when I feel conflicted about whether my work is important. It reassures me when I worry about becoming too self-absorbed in my work, to the exclusion of other important things in life.

When I was a young mom raising our four kids, it was clear there was no such thing as a true "work-life balance," a concept no previous generation ever dreamed of. My family's needs came first: that was the deal Jeff and I had made at the beginning of our marriage, and as the years went by and I watched our children grow, I was increasingly thankful we had made that choice. You can always revise and edit an article or book manuscript, but you can't go back and revise and edit your parenting mistakes. We all make them, even when you make motherhood Job #1, but I believed that my ability to be more present for the kids during their formative years would lead to fewer errors. I worked part-time while managing the house, cooking, shopping, preparing for Shabbat and holidays, driving carpool and taking the kids to all their appointments and activities. I exercised, attended Torah classes, and set aside a little quiet time with Jeff. I'd think, *When the kids are all grown up, I'll be able to work so much more!*

What was I smoking? Now as an older mom and grandmother of eleven, there's still no real work-life balance and there never will be. I still manage our home and am an active-duty Nana, spending time with our local grandkids and traveling a few times a year to visit the out-of-town kids and grandkids. At home, I also take many phone calls from my adult children, their spouses, or my husband. It's wonderful to have adult children and children-in-law who call to say hello, and who frequently ask my opinion about a child-rearing, life, or career issue. We Jewish mothers live for these moments. Why, we've spent decades developing and honing our perspectives to perfection! When others seek our advice, we are halfway up that stairway to heaven.

I have a friend who has five kids and runs a successful business from home. She guards her work hours with almost military precision and does not answer personal calls during work hours. What a woman! I admire her discipline. I've had trouble graduating from the mentality of my young mom days, when everyone else needed to come first, to the mentality of being an empty-nester professional who works at home and requires regular working hours.

A few years ago I decided that I could no longer be on call nearly all the time. I mustered my courage and with great fanfare announced to Jeff and the kids the hours when I would *not* be available, and my phone *would* be silenced. *So I'm not answering the phone if you call.* But I didn't leave the phone in another room. Some of my kids either forgot about this announcement or found it so foreign that it didn't register. When they still called during those work hours, it triggered a highly reactive and emotional mom response. Of course I answered.

Frankly, it wasn't possible to keep my rules inviolable. Two o'clock in Los Angeles was five o'clock on the east coast, the ideal time for me to read stories via FaceTime to my two-year-old grandson in Norfolk, Virginia. He ate a much heartier dinner when I read to him. Did I want a starving grandchild on my conscience? So I made another exception. My husband also runs a business and is extremely busy. He sometimes needs my help with an administrative task, often time-sensitive. Of course I'll stop my work to help. He's also likelier to text than to call, so when I see his name on the caller ID, sometimes I worry that there's a problem or perhaps he's not feeling well. I answer the call. What is it about the Jewish DNA that's always bracing for an emergency? It's not only work-life balance that's so elusive; it's the balance between my inflamed worry gene and *emuna*, the Jewish concept of feeling secure that God is running the show.

Shortly after writing a feature story about technology additions among children, based on Molly Frank's important book *Digital Detox*, I decided to ramp up my *emuna* and go for the obvious solution: ditch my phone during work hours. It no longer teased me by lying face down on silent mode inches from my hand because *I left it in another room.* This felt like I had sent it on a spaceship headed for a distant galaxy, or that I had just lopped off a vital appendage. That was proof of how desperately I needed to do this.

Our phones have monumentally complicated the boundaries between work and life. They've hobbled our ability to think without distractions, ratcheted up our anxieties, and made many of us tangibly unhappier. The more time we can wrench ourselves away from our phones during the day or evening, so much the better for us. I became much more productive and began to like the idea that I wasn't available every minute, even to the people I loved most in the world. Even those irresistible photos and videos of my grandchildren performing random acts of cuteness on our family WhatsApp could wait. This was small but important progress.

On Friday nights it is traditional for Jewish men to sing an ode to the Jewish woman, called *Eishet Chayil*, "A Woman of Valor." Praising the Jewish woman as nothing less than "a building block of creation," this poem is part of the Book of Proverbs, written by King Solomon. "A woman of valor, who can find? Far beyond pearls is her value. Her husband's heart trusts in her, and he shall lack no fortune." (Proverbs 31:1)

This somewhat mystical poem praises the seemingly endless achievements of one multitasking Jewish momma. She's a savvy businesswoman, negotiating real estate deals, weaving and selling linen garments, giving charity to the poor, making sure her family is well dressed and well fed, dispensing wisdom, and acting as a tower of strength for her husband and family. She sets the tone for kindness, personal growth, and spirituality not only in her family but in the community. It would never occur to this Eishet Chayil to worry about having enough time for self-care or whether she had nailed this work-life balance thing.

Our foremothers' lives were in many ways unrecognizable compared to our own, but as King Soloman's poem reveals, some things never change: as wives and mothers we will continue to juggle our duties as the days and nights—and the years—require. We are needed well into our children's adult lives, balancing our business lives while lending our emotional, intellectual, and spiritual support. And like the Eishet Chayil, we look to the future with confidence and good cheer.

From Generation to Generation

Grandchildren are the crown of their elders, and the glory of children is their parents.
—Proverbs 17:6

My writing life is imprinted with the love, encouragement, and influences of my four exceptionally different grandparents.

Cece demonstrated that women could become professionals in fields still dominated by men. Her decision to practice homeopathy and acupuncture when both seemed radical also modeled a thrilling independence of thinking and spirit. Perhaps most of all, her certainty that I would grow up to become a writer nourished that dream throughout my childhood and even my early adulthood.

Nana Cohen was a traditional Yiddishe *balabusta,* managing her household and supporting Papa Cohen in his work as a congregational rabbi, teacher, and scholar. With her ceaseless and voluble worry about our health, our connection to Judaism, and the safety of the Jewish people, she projected an uncomfortably perfect stereotype of a Jewish mother. I had sympathy, though. Nana grew up amid murderous anti-Semitism in Ukraine, and her worry had deep, authentic roots. Nana may have had a flair for melodrama, but she loved her family fiercely, and modeled a selfless commitment to building a loving Jewish home and performing acts of kindness.

Of all my grandparents, Papa Cohen had the most vibrant and instinctive writing gene. He left a trove of writing that—to my embarrassment—I only delved into decades after his passing. Among his hundreds of published articles, sermons, and recorded speeches on cassette tapes, I discovered several documents of archival value. I donated synagogue newsletters and conversion documents my grandfather signed during his years as the first congregational rabbi in Las Vegas to the University of Nevada, Las Vegas Library. A rare copy of a printed radio address from 1933 warning of the dangers of a rising Adolph Hitler, with Papa's handwritten notes on it, was accepted into the United States Holocaust Museum collection.

My paternal grandfather, Papa Rosenfeld, was also an eloquent man and had been a public speaker on behalf of the American Humanist Society. He wrote me only one letter during my whole life, one that taught me profound lessons about the power of words. In December 1971, nine months after Allan had died, Papa sent me this short, typed note on his personalized stationery:

> *Dear Judy,*
> *After doing much reading and thinking about the things that can affect you, I wanted to share one idea. The idea is this: that if we can learn to keep a smile on our face, the smile that grows out of a natural optimism, it will help us get through the rough patches in life. I believe this smile will not only help you but will spread to those around you.*
> *Much love,*
> *Silly Papa*

"Silly Papa" earned his nickname for the pranks and practical jokes he carried out with mischievous gusto. This letter was no joke. In fact, it was the only direct therapeutic message I received from anyone after our tragedy. No one in our family had the language of therapy, a field just beginning to become mainstream. I was a child of parents and grandparents who were expected to "stay strong and carry on," even as each of us stumbled, our hearts splintered in pain. Papa's letter let me know that he knew I was traumatized, but that there was hope for a happier tomorrow. That letter, which I later framed, became a kind of North Star for me.

Now, I try to pay this forward with my own grandchildren, trying to model the very best of my grandparents' legacies for them. I hope they see and feel my joy and gratitude from living a Torah-observant life, one they might come to take for granted because they will not have known anything else growing up.

Naturally, I share my love of good writing and my belief in the power of words with them, through reading to them and cheering their early efforts in writing. When I sit with my grandchildren, often reading the same dog-eared books I read to their parents, my delight truly knows no bounds.

One Shabbat afternoon when I was laid up in bed with a terrible headache, my ten-year-old granddaughter, Ahuva, came to my room to visit. She eyed the book I had at my side, *84, Charing Cross Road*, a little gem of a memoir in letters. It's a classic that I had loved for decades, and I was about to read it again.

"Would you like me to read it to you?" I asked, hopeful.

She nodded enthusiastically, and for the next half hour the two of us sat snugly together on the bed, transported back to 1948, when letters flew back and forth between New York writer Helene Hanff and London bookseller Frank Doel, who specialized in rare and out of print books. Over twenty years, their correspondence blossomed into a true friendship. I needed to explain several things, such as the concept of food rationing, the difference between poetry and prose, and what made vellum binding so special. This was a good opportunity to show her our century-old leather-bound set of Jane Austen, which we had bought at an antiquarian book fair. I carefully pulled *Mansfield Park* off the shelf and let Ahuva feel the smooth, soft mocha-hued leather cover and touch its faded but still beautiful pages. "Once upon a time, many books were made this way," I explained.

As we continued to read, my granddaughter began to recognize the power of small details in the story, and we both laughed at the author's brusque and flippant humor. As I had found with my own kids, reading to independent readers is a precious opportunity, one more crucial point of connection in a society whose digital addictions damage attention spans and fracture relationships.

Who is likely to read your words? Who might be touched by them, and perhaps share them with a friend, a sister, or a grandchild? Papa Rosenfeld wrote his three-sentence letter to an audience of one—his ten-year-old granddaughter. Yet for more than fifty years, that note reinforced my foundation of hope and optimism, something I have been privileged to share with hundreds of thousands of readers. Papa's precious note taught me that what we write may have potential beyond anything we might realize.

Acknowledgments

Many people have been part of this book's journey and it's time to thank them. Sun Cooper and Howard Lovy both saw the potential in my blog series, "Chasing the Byline," to blossom into a full-bodied book and provided invaluable guidance. Jill Kahn, friend and life coach, showed me how to tap into my courage and get the writing done. Thank you to my beta readers Linda Abraham, David Altschuler, Emma Fialkoff, Jessica Keet, Denise Koek, Jennifer Lawler, Jill Moray Reichman, Karen Rinehart, Mark Schiff, and Laura Weinman. Your enthusiasm and recommendations were gratefully welcomed. To Carol Bradley, a long-standing sister in the book writing trenches, thank you for the weekly check-ins and the camaraderie. Niva Taylor has assisted me for several years, editing my manuscripts, helping me with book promotional efforts, and designing my website, all with great skill. Nechemia Coopersmith, editor in chief of *Aish.com* and David Suissa, publisher and editor in chief of *The Jewish Journal* have provided a home for my work for many years, letting my writing reach a wide audience. Huge thanks to the team at Koehler Books: John Koehler, Becky Hilliker, Danielle Koehler, and Adrienne Folkerts. My book has been in great hands!

My family is the source of my most precious blessings. Avi and Aliza, Noach and Esty, Ben and Rivka, and Yael and Yonah (and all your kids, to whom this book is dedicated): thank you for your excitement for this project and gracious indulgence when you find yourselves unexpectedly in my copy, even though you don't really have a choice. My husband, Jeff, has supported my writing efforts in every way from the beginning, and also made wise editing suggestions. His support for me personally and professionally continues to make all the difference.

Finally and above all, I thank the Almighty for all His blessings, including each already mentioned, and for guiding me toward this meaningful, joy-filled, path as a Jewish writer.

About the Author

Judy Gruen is the author of the acclaimed memoir *The Skeptic and the Rabbi: Falling in Love with Faith* and several other books. Her humor title *The Women's Daily Irony Supplement* won Foreword INDIE's Gold Award and Independent Publisher's Silver Award for humor. A columnist and book reviewer for the *Jewish Journal*, she has also written for the *Wall Street Journal, Chicago Tribune, Boston Globe, Los Angeles Times, Woman's Day, Christian Science Monitor,* Aish.com, *Jewish Action*, and other media outlets.

Judy's insightful and personal writing about life as a proudly observant Jewish woman in a secular society has earned her a wide following. She earned her bachelor's degree in English from UC Berkeley and her master's degree in journalism from Northwestern University. Judy lives in Los Angeles with her husband, Jeff.

Learn more at judygruen.com.

www.ingramcontent.com/pod-product-compliance
Lightning Source LLC
LaVergne TN
LVHW041935070526
838199LV00051BA/2799